Poetic Inspirations

Mission: To Proclaim Transformation and Truth

Publisher: Transformed Publishing, Cocoa, Florida
Website: www.transformedpublishing.com
Email: transformedpublishing@gmail.com

Copyright © 2021 by Babette Bailey

All rights reserved solely by the author. No part of this book may be reproduced, stored in a retrieval system, or transmitted in any form or by any means without expressed written permission of the author.

All author work was submitted to the publisher as original work.

ISBN: 978-1-953241-24-5 Paperback

Poetic Inspirations

Original Poems by: Babette Bailey

Foreword

I enjoy writing poetry, and the different ventures I get to take in my imagination, in my heart, my experiences, my dreams, and even the lives and experiences of many others. I believe poems are the beginnings, or the seeds of stories, movies, songs and even new directions. I know how they can inspire, just like a song, or someone's testimony of some of the amazing things they've gone through, and the next thing you know, new adventures and exciting new journeys have begun.

I hope I can inspire you to read each poem with anticipation of where each journey could take you, or what spark it can ignite in you; what new adventure it will inspire you to take; and even what dream can be jumpstarted in you to make you begin to strive again for something you've longed for or longed to do.

Many times, when I'm writing, I can see a picture of the events happening in my mind. I've laughed and even cried with emotion as I'm filled with the pain and the joy of each experience as I put myself right in the center of it all. I've felt the anticipation and the excitement in my own mind of what would happen next; and I've even been lifted in my heart as I write and create, dream, and go places I may never go except in my mind.

I believe we all have a creative mind, as we are made in the image of God, the ultimate Creator of everything. And I believe it is for all of us, the birthplace of greatness and miracles, and amazing and wonderful new journeys and experiences.

I hope you will come and that you will enjoy sharing in these poetic inspirations with me, and that you will be inspired to tap into and release your own creative abilities.

Acknowledgments:

Once again, I'm very thankful to God for giving me the dreams, and allowing me the opportunity to see my dreams being fulfilled; also to all of you who encourage me and support the dreams, the visions, the gifts, the talents, and even the desires God has given me to not just write, but to share my heart and experiences with as many as I can who are willing, who are open, and who understand that without others to share our dreams, they don't mean half as much.

I want to acknowledge and say thanks once again to my paternal and spiritual family and close friends, and to all those past and present who have inspired myself and many others to write, to create, to dare to reach for our dreams, and then to share with the world.

Thanks to my publisher who has helped me beyond what she has been paid by teaching me and helping me by investing in my efforts to learn and even be able to put together the writings myself; encouraging me to grow and learn and expand, even to share on social media and other community events and opportunities.

I appreciate more than I can say all those that care enough to say it and do enough to show it. I heard someone say once, and I'm paraphrasing, that it is not selfish to reach for our dreams and share them; or to strive to be all that we can be. It's selfish not to. With that, I'm striving to be as unselfish as I can, with hopefully and prayerfully more and more to come, to the glory of God.

Table of Contents

1. That Still Small Voice
2. What God Joins Together
3. 80 Years Strong
4. Sporting Them Natural Locks
5. Straight Purity
6. I Won't
7. Intentionally Broken
8. Finally You
9. A Brand New Start
10. A Taste of da Diaspora
11. When We Are No More
12. What A Privilege
13. In My Eyes
14. Listen And Consider
15. Making Disciples
16. Thinking of Love
17. The Glory of God
18. The Enemies Within
19. Forward And Beyond
20. Questions
21. The Dreams
22. That's What It Did For Me
23. A Welcoming Change
24. Christmas Demands
25. My Mind, My Soul, My Body
26. Got To Change
27. Hope Revealed
28. His Peace
29. Greatness
30. Remembering Special Times With Our Mothers
34. Unique And Special Roses Collection
41. Next Chapter
42. Lifting Us
43. No Matter What
44. Walter (AKA June Bug)
45. Thanks Goes With Giving
46. Check Your Heart
47. Destination Greatness
48. Through The Tests And Trials
49. Your Race

Table of Contents

50. Considering Christmas
51. Singing Praises To God
52. Longing
53. What Does It Look Like?
54. I've Been There, Done That
55. Awaken, Rise And Shine
56. Awaken
57. Hope Fading
58. Getting Ready
59. Royal Robes
60. Rare And Special
61. Few Are Chosen
62. Happy Anniversary
63. Celebrating 50 Years
64. Yes We Can
65. I Wanna See You Soar
66. Can You Drink That Cup
67. We Need You
68. Women On The Front Lines
69. The Game
70. Sister Girl
71. The 6th Man
72. Words of Encouragement
73. The Brother Was Right
74. God's Saving Grace
75. God Gets The Glory
76. My Cross
77. Take That Bully Out
78. Don't You Wanna Go
79. The Way
80. Laughter
81. Men That Matter
82. Good News
83. Tied Up, Tangled Up, Wrapped Up
84. Get Ready
85. An Even Greater Call
86. Love, Tell Me Where You Are
87. Cover Us
88. Additional Words
89. Original Poetic Calendars Order Information

Babette Bailey

That Still Small Voice

Look not always where the crowds are or where everyone seems to be going
Don't always be concerned at how fierce the winds, but consider what the calmness is showing
When the earth quakes don't settle because of fear, don't run cause you're looking at man
But listen for that still small voice of God that speaks like no one else can

I believe the reason Jesus is so effective in everything He does
Is because He genuinely and wholeheartedly loves and cares for all of us
Take a good look at love and consider what amazing things love can do
Consider the effects of real love and how real love can soothe

They say a baby if it's not held within so many hours after birth it will die
Not from bad health or being malnourished, but from the longing for what love provides
Love can cheer a heavy heart and give the hopeless the courage to dream
Love can cause the sick to refuse to give up and be healed miraculously
Love can break the chains of overwhelming pain, from emotional and physical abuse
Love can bring forth a joy and fulfillment like nothing else in this world can do
Love can give peace to a tormented soul and shine light in the darkest places
Love can rebuild, restore, revive, rekindle and transform in amazing ways
Take you places you never dreamed you go, fill a void so wide and so deep
Even when it seems utterly impossible, one drop of love can turn bitter to sweet
It can make the ugliest things beautiful, with patience and kindness and time
Love can take away suffering and pain, prejudice, selfishness and pride

When you don't have a clue, can't see your way
Trouble surrounding and you feel dismayed
Hopeless and discouraged, doubtful and sad
Confused and lonely, overwhelmed and mad
Don't give up and don't throw in the towel
Don't give up the fight, but hold on somehow
And listen for that still small voice again
That voice that's soft but speaks volumes

What God Joins Together

This man and this woman that God is crowning today
Joining their lives in holy matrimony making vows to love always
He says he'll forever be faithful, cherish and treat her kind
She says she's ready and willing to submit as his loving wife

Now what God joins together let no one ever tear apart
What God has said let be, forever be joined in their hearts
If this love is destined to be and God has given His blessing
Let joy and the hope of love last forever, let it always be fulfilling

It's a beautiful thing when a man finds a woman and he's ready to give his heart
It's wonderful because she feels the same way, and they never want to be apart
It's a big step they know, but they believe they have God's yes
They believe that with God on their sides their marriage will be blessed

They're believing God to be their guide and to be with them every day
They're ready to proclaim their love to the world, ready for that special day
They're ready to have and to hold, richer or poorer, sickness or health
Good times or bad, happy or sad, they feel that they cannot fail

To pray together, dream together, overcome all the odds and tests
Accept each others' weaknesses and flaws even when they're not at their best
By faith they forsake all others and join together in holy matrimony
By faith they receive the favor of God; by faith they will succeed

Babette Bailey

80 Years Strong

Number 5 out of 9 children born to her mom and dad
Who would have thought 80 years later she could have accomplished all that she has

Born in a little town in Florida, a place called White Springs
As a child, worked in the fields, and had her share of cotton picking

Played basketball, and could run, held her own back in the day
Could sew, could sing, and could cook too, all at a very young age

Destined to care for children, she had 10 children of her own
Cared for all the grands and great-grands too, till they were almost grown

I remember when we were growing up, she would carry her leather strap
Every now and then she'd surprise you, and get your attention with a good little tap

It would always catch you by surprise because she would threaten you again and again
And there was no way of telling when she had reached that point where there was no more warning

I know that there were hard times, but I don't recall her ever breaking
The things that stand out in my mind were gospel music, cooking and cleaning

When I think of my mother's strength, I think of the pioneers
Enduring and persevering, whatever the conditions and no place or time for tears

Always caring for others, always giving and always kind
Is just who she is and what she does, she couldn't change if she tried

She's 80 years strong but still handling her own, still pressing though time has taken its toll
She's starting to show signs that she's fragile and weak now from years of refusing to grow old

Sporting Them Natural Locks

Yau'll ladies sporting them natural locks
Them curls looking good, yau'll done stepped out the box

Yau'll done spoiled the devil's plans, he thought he had this thing sold
He never expected you to be so confident and so bold

But just like the Good News, the Word has gotten out
And it's spreading like a wildfire from the North to the South

Some still aren't quite ready, some say never naturale
Then there are some like me, we stepped out but we fell

But none can deny yau'll sisters are looking great
Yau'll have started a mighty movement and you're gracefully leading the way

I believe this thing is prophetic, the truth has set you free
Now God is using you for the nations, to exhort, encourage and teach

And the more others see how God is moving and transforming your lives
The more are drawn to that life changing truth, that will help them and open their eyes

So, continue to let those natural locks shine, believe me the world is looking
So, keep boldly, confidently, gracefully and eloquently displaying that God-given, natural beauty

Babette Bailey

Straight Purity

Purity is like a newborn baby, not yet tainted, still innocent and clean
Never heard, spoken, looked upon, imagined, never touched an unclean thing

Purity is choosing to be set apart for a special time and a special place
To preserve, to treasure, to cherish and safeguard to keep till that very special day

So, as you make your purity vows today, embrace the choice that you've made
Not only have you chosen the better life, you've chosen the better way

But on the real yo straight purity! Staying pure gonna have you down on your knees
You've got to pray if you're gonna stay pure, you won't do it without calling on Jesus

You think temptation is just some word? No, that demon of temptation is real
I'm not saying God isn't greater, but that flesh always wants what it feels

But purity is honorable and rewarding, you can expect God's best for your obedience
You're definitely making the right choice, much respect to you for taking this stance

Look around there's some men you can look up to, there's some virtuous women to be admired
They've made the same choices that you're making as you look at them may you be inspired

As you place your minds and give your heart and commit your bodies to the Lord
I believe God is pleased and smiling on you, I believe you can be assured

But once again, yo straight purity! Means you've got to wait till you say I do
You're gonna need to be strapped ever day with the full armor of God to keep you

A guard for both of your eyes, both of your ears and both of your hands
You're gonna need guards for your heart and mind; you lose them there's no way you can stand

I Won't

I won't be down, I won't be blue
I won't be discouraged, I won't be moved
I won't be sad, I'm not gonna cry
I won't, because Jesus is on my side

I won't be depressed, I won't wear a frown
I won't be oppressed or pushed around
I won't give up, I won't be denied
I won't, because Jesus is the Lord of my life

I won't be afraid, I won't run away
I won't be intimidated, I won't go astray
I won't be pushed out, or pushed aside
I won't because Jesus is my guide

I won't be fooled, I won't be dismayed
I won't be silly, I won't go my own way
I won't be hopeless, I won't be denied
I won't because Jesus has paid the price

He said if He be for me
Who could be against me
If He gives me His favor
How can I be defeated
If He's my rock and shield
I won't fail because that's not His will

Intentionally Broken

Nothing beautiful to look upon
Not attractive to the eyes of man
Grieved and full of sorrows, despised and rejected
He was broken without and from within
He carried the weight of the world in His heart
He was crucified and pierced in His side
For our rebellion He was beaten
For our transgressions gave His life
They laid a crown of thorns on His head
He never complained though the pain overwhelming
All the punishment, oppression and loneliness
He endured intentionally
Who can begin to comprehend a love so great
As the love He gave
How can we begin to understand
The amazing price that Jesus paid
Let us take some time to think on the cost
Some time to reflect on His amazing grace
Think of the wrongs that we have done
And all the ways that He has made
Then imagine God giving His only Son
Granting us the forgiveness to start anew
He sacrificed, He paid it all
All was to say - I Love You!

Finally You

I think I finally realized that God loves me
I think I've finally opened my eyes and I can see
That I can rest in His love, in His promises because
I realize God is faithful and His love is free

I've been trying so hard to earn God's love
Doing all I can so His love will never leave
Afraid of failing, or making the wrong move
Going out of my mind cause I really couldn't see

Trying to show Him my love cause I need Him so much
Trying to serve and give my best to earn His love
Doing all I've heard and seen to be strong and sin free
I didn't realize that even then He still loves me

God's love is renewing me, molding me and changing me
God's love is maturing me, washing me and cleansing me
God knows I'm not perfect & that's why He's so patient
That's why He's so forgiving and in His love I find rest

Doesn't mean things will always be easy
Doesn't mean I won't ever go through
Doesn't mean I'm better than anyone else
Doesn't mean I don't have work to do

Babette Bailey

A Brand New Start

Hey brothers, mind if I share with you
Something that's been on my heart
Something I hope will possibly enable us
Both to have a brand new start
From a single woman, a single mother
I sure could use your help
I'm not ashamed to say it any longer
It's time to put that pride on the shelf
I'm struggling, not just financially
But trying to do everything on my own
And I sure could use someone to hold me
And help me when all my strength is gone
Won't you please think about and consider
How much you have that I need
God made us to help each other
Alone we're both incomplete
I know women can be complicated
But I'm willing to give my best try
I'm ready to serve, to submit and stop nagging
I'm getting my life right with Christ
Would you love me, cover me and protect me
And not take advantage of my weakness
You're a man of God, so I know you understand
That to be weaker doesn't mean to be less

A Taste of da Diaspora

Somebody said oh taste and see
Dat da Lord our God is good
He is good in da dance, good in da song
And as da say in Jamaica, good in de food

We have come from many backgrounds
Many nations and many lands
But our roots are still deeply tied
To da place where it all began

We have different flavors, cultures
Different colors and pedigrees
But we're all tied to da Creator
To da One dat created every tings

We have come to share expressions
Of who we are and our ancestral roots
As we offer you a taste of da diaspora
We introduce to you

Jamaica, West Africa, Honduras, Puerto Rico
USA, Trinidad and Tobago and dares more
So let your imaginations and taste buds explore
Come, join us on dis journey; come let's travel and taste de world

Babette Bailey

When We Are No More

Many years are now behind us, and the view ahead has definitely changed
We used to see with desires and expectations, but now we see with heartfelt thanks
For many there is fear and dread, as they can't help but look forward in time
But with all we've dared and all we've discovered, we've learned how to fight and survive
We've laughed and cried, but we've always held on
We've danced and heard the melodies of the most beautiful songs
We've sacrificed and stood and seen much in this life
We've left our prints in this world, and we've shined our lights
We're okay with tomorrow, all our doubts and worries have been erased
By all the wonders and the amazement we've seen in our yesterdays
The kids say we don't want to talk about that now
But we tell them it's okay
For when we are no more
They will see what we see today
They'll always have special memories
That will bring a smile or a tear
They'll always have the thoughts that can make a loved one
Seem like they are near
We can't ignore there will definitely come a time
When we are all no more
So we prepare, ourselves and appreciate each other
And embrace the todays much more
Now is the time for sharing our hearts
And getting our houses in order
Getting right with God, neighbors and family
And making sure we settle every score
Say I'm sorry and forgive those we need to
Make amends and do all we can
Then rest knowing when we are no more
Our stories will have a happy end

What A Privilege

What A privilege Lord to know You
To be chosen by You; kept by You
Protected by You; loved by You
Blessed by You
What a privilege to receive You

What A privilege Lord to come to You
To seek after You; cast our cares on You
To call on You; to be touched by You
To be filled by You
What a privilege all that You do

What A privilege Lord to feel Your grace
What a privilege Lord to know Your name
What a privilege Lord to know all You've done
What a privilege Lord You giving us Your Son

What A privilege Lord to sing Your praises
Every day we have to give You thanks
To know Your ways; to hear You say
To be covered by Your amazing grace
What a privilege Lord to worship only You

Babette Bailey

In My Eyes

My eyes see you predestined to be
And called from your mother's womb
Shaped and sculptured by the hands of God
Submitted for His use
You're equally yoked and a powerful team
You compliment each other so well
In my eyes, your hearts are passionate and sincere
Toward God and everyone else
You've been set apart, you're unique and you're rare
Your enduring and your labor shows how much you care
You're humble, your hearts are made of flesh, not of stone
In my eyes I see that your life's not your own
Your legacy will speak, long after you're gone
For your words, your voices we hear when we're alone
Resounding, reminding, and reassuring what you teach
In my eyes you're practicing just what you preach
I can feel your hearts sharing our pain
Your actions of goodness always displayed
I see depth and volume, intensity and fire
In my eyes, I see in you things I admire
Who am I to tell you what my thoughts are of you
For you know who you are and you're doing what you do
But if it's any consolation in me sharing a glimpse of my heart
In my eyes you're a reflection of our Bright and Morning Star
You're a glimpse of His glory
You're an extension of His hand
You're a sample of His goodness
Your light shines in the land
You're not looking for praise
But I applaud what you do
May the investment you're making be given back to you

Listen And Consider

If you're made in His image, what do you do
Don't neglect to receive the help of those reaching for you
Take a moment to consider, has your shoes or your clothes worn out
Through your wilderness, through your struggles, have you thought of turning around
Egypt may seem easier, going back to being slaves
But not when you believe that Jesus is the way
The suffering will develop you, and after you suffer a while
You'll be complete, lacking nothing, your frown will become a smile
What I'm trying to say in all this is hold on and be strong
Don't murmur, don't complain and don't provoke God living wrong
Learn from the children of Israel, learn from where you've failed
Learn from people who have seen and experienced glimpses of heaven & hell
Trust and believe in the all mighty God, don't let go, taste and see
He's a wonderful, faithful and loving Father, He really has everything we need
Like the children in the wilderness, I've murmured and complained
I didn't see all that I had received, or how I had been sustained
All I cared and thought about were the things that I desired
Not having them and longing so long made others seem like liars
I couldn't see how God was caring for me
I couldn't see His protection and provision for me
I didn't understand love unconditionally
But God was waiting for me patiently
I didn't have a clue, I was in darkness and deceived
But God was there before I knew Him, faithful indeed
He's faithful to His promises in spite of what we do
We can lean on Him and depend on Him, no matter what we're going through
He has a promised land, the land of milk and honey
Where we have all we need, and can buy without money
If only we can trust His help
Let go and let Him order our steps

Making Disciples

Making disciples for the saving of souls
Equipping those who are willing to go

Fulfilling hearts and fulfilling minds
With the wisdom and the understanding of Christ

Guiding in love and guiding in grace
Humbly serving and leading the way

Imparting power, imparting faith
Encouraging and empowering day by day

Building leaders and building teams
Strengthening followers who will one day lead

Travailing in power for those who are called
Love expressed from the Lover of all

Preparing disciples for the journey is a must
Ensuring, enduring and emphasizing trust

Uprooting fear and tearing down pride
Exposing the troubles buried inside

You sow, you water, you nurture, you train
You're equipping more that more can be saved

Thinking of Love

Thinking of love and what I would say
I remember hearing a song one day
That what the world needs now is love sweet love
That it's the only thing there's just too little of
And as I've searched for love and wondered about love
I agree indeed there's just not enough
Oh there's enough lust and enough desire
There are even enough people that we can admire
But we need more of what love is meant to be
More patience, more kindness, more heartfelt deeds
More of God's love, loving God's way
That life giving love, that changes things
Yes, Jesus has shown us what love really is
How sacrificing ourselves means others can live
For He received the most, when He gave His all
Showed us sacrificing is the greatest call
So don't withhold extending your hand
Don't expect others to meet your demands
Don't focus on self, but on those who need help
Don't hide your love, or put it on a shelf
You can't beat God's giving, no matter how you try
What we give we always get back multiplied

Babette Bailey

The Glory of God

It's been a long time coming, but I still believe
That I'm going to see what He showed to me
It's been a little while since God showed me the dream
But I still believe that it will be

I've had to go through some trials, had to endure some pain
But God is faithful I've come to believe
I know the tests and pain I've endured along the way
Will work for my good and His glory

I know I have to walk by faith, so I fight the good fight of faith
Others have doubt, even family and friends, but God has the final say

It's not by my power, not by my might, but it's all by the power in His hands
That's what keeps me strong, keeps the fire burning, and keeps me trusting His plan

He said stand still and in the due season, that He would reveal His glory
I believe He's able to do exceedingly, abundantly above what we can ask or think

I refuse to give up or be moved; so I'm standing on what I believe
I'm standing on His promises, I won't let go until I receive

The Enemies Within

We think of our enemies as people we don't like, and people who don't like us
They're people we'd never invite to our homes, be close to or ever trust
Usually those who don't like us, don't have a problem letting us know
But there are enemies we don't recognize, because they've gotten so close
They're called the enemies within; they're called lovers, family and friends
They're the ones that can do the most harm, because we have let down our guard
The damage can be life threatening, even fatal depending on the circumstances
Either way the damage can be more than enough to devastate all other chances
We've heard the military can have spies within; those that would sell out their own country
We've seen how spouses can turn on each other; go from lovers to fighting as enemies
We've seen good families fall apart, business partners suing each other
Church members falling out with each other; those who call themselves brothers
There's another enemy we often miss; another who we least expect
That's the enemy within ourselves; it's our own hurt we fail to detect
Have you ever told yourself you can't do it; have you ever told yourself you can't win
Have you lied to yourself or put yourself down; do you hurt yourself by the way you live
So many lives have been devastated; because we fail to acknowledge these truths
I'm not saying don't trust, don't love, don't live; but beware of the enemies in you
Be sober, be vigilant, be prayerful; know that the devil will use who he can
He can get into the heart and mind to destroy and hurt any man
The enemy will lie and deceive you; he will do all he can to mislead you
But there's one who is always for you; Jesus Christ, who died for you

Forward And Beyond

Anybody ready to make that big move; ready to go forward and beyond
Ready to break barriers, ready to see miracles, ready to step up and stand on
Get your tools and get your instructions; if you believe it's time to break ground
If there are things you're ready to discover; if you can hear that distinctive sound

Forward and beyond to things you've never seen, places you've never been, people you've yet to meet
Opportunities and new discoveries; new inventions amazing and great things
You've been praying and you've been searching, you've been hoping and you've believed
You've sacrificed and you've paid the price; now it's time to unveil those dreams

Eyes have not seen, ears have not heard what God has in store for us
For those who love Him and worship Him; for those who would give Him their trust
Have you ever gone beyond the deep blue sea; seen the wonderful things beyond the deep
Can you imagine the colors, the awe, the journey; can you imagine you being all you long to be

The sky is the limit; there are mountains to be conquered
There are new foods to be tasted, and new songs to be heard
Can you see yourself moving forward, soaring high up in the skies
See God's amazing mysteries unfolding before your very eyes

Take the steps, take the chance, take your eyes off your circumstance
Hold God's hands, trust His plan; let Him guide you to the promised land
Walk by faith, walk God's way; follow His steps as He paves the way
Go beyond; look beyond what others have to say

God has another level of wonder; new dimensions, and new heights
New sights unimaginable, awesome things that will blow your mind
The dreams of a lifetime; your hopes and desires
Forward and beyond; to the journey of your life

Poetic Inspirations

Questions

Frustrated, discouraged and disappointed
Over and over again
Fighting with anyone
And everyone you feel that's boxing you in
This void you've been trying to fill
Can't be filled by just a man
Man without God is limited
Even when he's doing all he can
There's a void that nothing can satisfy
Apart from the Spirit of God
Sacrifice and more
Cannot satisfy apart from the Almighty One
Even with good intentions and an all out effort to love
All your might and all your strength, still is not enough
You can carry great loads and go a long way
You can only give so much, and only so much you can take
The questions may still go unanswered
The challenges may seem unending
The longing like it'll never be fulfilled
The burdens may feel overwhelming
Lest God build and watch over you
Your labor will always be in vain
Lest you invite God in the midst of your life
You'll continue to go through the pain
So, the questions that you must now ask
Is how to press through and fight the good fight
How to tap into the Spirit of God
How to love Him with all your might

The Dreams

What if you believed in what God has given to me
The dream and seemingly impossible things He told me could be
What if you stood and believed with me the plan He has for my life
Though the dream is much bigger than me, and it's not by my power or might
I remember when Joseph had a dream, he knew that it came from God
His brothers never considered it could be, they didn't give it a second thought
Then with all the other trials and distractions, the disappointments and the wait
I imagine that Joseph may have doubted it too, especially as things were delayed
But in one hour he went from the prison to the palace and those dreams came to be
Got turned things around and before they knew it, his brothers would also see
I'm also reminded of David, never once was he considered to be king
As Samuel looked at all David's brothers in David he didn't see anything
But none of his brothers were chosen
David had been undoubtedly set apart by God
Everyone had looked at his outer appearance
But God knew the depth of his heart
I'm convinced that God has something just for me
Cause the dreams inside just won't fade
I've tried to fulfill them and tried to measure up
But I realize I can't do it my way
I cannot manipulate anything, I tried to make it happen in my time
But I've come to understand that God's will must ultimately become mine
So I'm striving to stand like Joseph and to occupy like David in the field
Trusting, believing, worshiping
Giving everything I have to do His will
Sometimes it feels like God is running late
Looking at my clock
Wondering and praying God how long
The wait, the longing, the expectation
Makes it feel like something's wrong
But God will bring the dreams to pass
He'll prepare us for that special day
He knows when we are ready and equipped for the dreams
He will fulfill them in His time and in His way

That's What It Did For Me

I didn't know how to forgive
Forgiveness just didn't make sense
I didn't even want to forgive
All I could think of was how great the offense
But I asked the Lord to show me how
Since it was His idea in the first place
I asked Him to help me out
To show me how to extend His grace
To my amazement, it happened so fast
The pain and the anger were gone
I couldn't help but wonder if the peace would last
But I knew I hadn't done it on my own
I believe that God could see my heart
A heart to trust Him and to obey
I didn't even know how bound up I was
Till He took all those chains away
It felt good to be free of the hatred
The anger, the hurt and the rage
I felt a weight lifted off of me
I felt clean and ready to embrace
I even found myself laughing
That's when I knew my heart was made clean
Now I know to forgive is to be free
Because that's what it did for me

A Welcoming Change

God told Zaccheus to come down immediately
He would stay at his house that day
Zaccheus came down and welcomed Jesus gladly
Something in Zaccheus had changed
The people thought Jesus had made a mistake
Going to the house of a well-known sinner
But soon it was clear that God had seen something
Beyond Zaccheus' darkened exterior
Can you imagine Jesus coming to your house to stay?
Is He invited? Would you welcome Him in?
Can He look into your heart? Can He see the change?
Can He see what others can't comprehend?
If you're getting your heart ready and renewing your mind
God sees past where you are today
He knows those whose hearts are turned to Him
He knows those who are ready for change
Don't stop reaching. Don't stop striving
God can show up any time in our lives
Don't grow weary. Your labor is not in vain.
What you're giving, you'll reap in due time
The benefits are not just for you or me
God can bless a multitude with our seed
Let's expect God to do exceedingly and abundantly
Above what we can ask or think
As we prepare our hearts and invite Jesus in
Let's expect God to fulfill His Word
He said He'd give us the desires of our hearts
If we'd delight ourselves in Him first
So let's keep believing, keep seeking, keep hoping
For all His promises are ours to embrace
Let's keep loving, pressing, praying and giving
Till we see God's welcoming change

Christmas Demands

Twas just days before Christmas
Everybody's making their Christmas plans
What they want to give, where they want to go
Caught up in all the Christmas demands
Preparing for the parties, get-togethers and plays
Luncheons and family gatherings, and how long their gonna stay
Pulling out the decorations and dressing the trees
Christmas cards and carolers and favorite recipes
Each of our favorite versions of Silent Night
Those memorable classics and movies everybody likes
But wait a minute hold up, something just ain't right
There's the hype and all that, but what about the True Light
Are we really exalting the King with a heartfelt praise
Are we really bringing honor and glory to His name
Is His light shining brightly for all to see
Are we filled in our hearts the way we should be
With love and joy, gratitude and peace
Goodness and kindness and the faith to believe
As you share with your family, friends and more
I pray that you'll remember what this season is for
I pray that the light of Jesus Christ will shine bright
I pray that His joy will be felt in every life
I pray that the songs will bring more than just cheer
I pray that all will feel the comfort of knowing He is near
I pray He'll be pleased with the love as we share
The warmth we display and how much we care
Remember the Gift God has given to us
The greatest blessing, the greatest love
As Christmas demands our lights to shine
Don't forget the True Light is Jesus Christ

Babette Bailey

My Mind, My Soul, My Body

Yeah I like the beat, the melody is sweet
Sounds good to me, makes me move in my seat

But the praise comes from my heart, my praise is unto God
I praise Him with every part of me, my mind, my soul and my body

Yeah I like the groove, the melody is smooth
Makes me wanna bust a move, makes me feel like dancing too

But I worship from my heart, my worship is to God
I worship with every part of me, my mind, my soul, and my body

Yes, love is my ambition, love is my intention
Love is my guide & direction, love is the real connection

The reason why I dance, the reason I lift my hands
The reason I take my stand, the reason I give Him all I can

My love is unto God, love that's from my heart
I love God with every part of me, my mind, my soul and my body

One more thing, if you like to sing, if you have faith, and if you believe
If you know that Jesus is really the King and that He is Lord of everything

Then sing to Him with all your heart, sing your praises unto God
Sing to Him with every part of you, your mind, your soul and your body

Got To Change

You've got to change your ways
You've got make the change
You've got to submit to God
Everything in your heart
If you want to see God's blessings
There are some special conditions
Resist the enemy
Trust God and believe
Get wisdom and understanding
And that's just the beginning
Give Him quality time
Make the sacrifice
Learn to be still and wait
Learn to watch as you pray
Let Him guide you every day
Seek Him, and His Way
Seek His righteousness
Trust that you will be blessed
Walk by faith, not by what you think
Believe without seeing
For His thoughts are not like ours
For He has all power
What He says will be
He rules everything

Babette Bailey

Hope Revealed

Hope revealed is when your young adult calls you and tells you
They're going to church with you on Sunday
Or when the job you interviewed for calls you back and asks you
If you can start on Monday
It's when the doctor says he can't explain your improvement
But there's no more signs or symptoms
It's when you can get those pants up over your hips
And almost get them fastened
It's when he takes you to dinner, his hands are sweaty
Because he's holding a little black box
Or when that thing you've been praying for goes on sale
And you got a little extra in your paycheck
It's when the whale that swallowed you releases you
And spits you back up on dry land
Or you feel that strong arm of God directing you
And lifting you up with His hands
It's when God goes before you years ahead
To make a way for you to be preserved
It's even when you know you've done wrong but He blesses you
Even though you don't deserve it
Hope revealed is when you see the flashing lights
You pull over, but they go on ahead
It's when that problem you've been trying to resolve
Begins to be a blessing to you instead
It's when one person decides to yield
And goes to the other to say I'm sorry
Or when you feel the peace of God transcending
The fear, the hurt and the worry
It's when you want to ask her out, as your thinking of how
She starts looking and heading your way
Or you're called to go before the King
And God gives you just the right words to say
Hope is revealed when we know what God says
And we determine to walk by faith
Trusting, waiting, enduring, believing
No matter what comes your way
Hope revealed is when we really realize
That Jesus died for our sins
It's when we receive His grace, His love, His promises
And our peace returns to us again

Poetic Inspirations

His Peace

The reason God gives us peace
Is to encourage us not to give up hope
To keep our eyes fixed upon Him
And our emotions under control
To help us think soberly and clearly
So we won't be overtaken and consumed
Not by fear not by anxiety
Not by hopelessness or gloom
To help us stand in the midst of trouble
To help us through life's toil and pain
To show us His Word and His promises are true
And He will always make a way
Jesus never worried nor panicked
He trusted God and His Word
He took every situation to the Father in prayer
He stayed in peace by keeping God first
Knowing God was with Him
Gave Him confidence to speak to the wind
Knowing and walking in the purpose of God
Helped Him endure till the end
He wasn't ignorant of the wiles of the devil
He never relied on human strength
He was always focused on the plan of God
Because the plan of God was His sole intent
He told us He would keep us in perfect peace
If we would keep our minds stayed on Him
He showed us by example in the way He lived
Over and over again
His peace surpasses all understanding
His peace gives us hope
His peace gives us assurance
And leads us calmly through the unknown

Greatness

When baby Jesus was born
God had greatness purposed for His life
Even from a baby many could see
He was extraordinary and He was divine
God created man in His image
He filled us with greatness to glorify His name
He gave us talent, inspiration, gifts, passion
And the ability to do great things
We've seen many great accomplishments and successes
Amazing and unbelievable things
We've seen hopeless situations and tragedies
Turn into great opportunities
We were inspired as children, we had hopes and dreams
Of the great things that we would do
Those were seeds of greatness, the beginnings of
The great things God would see us through
Greatness starts in our hearts and minds
And often looks impossible to achieve
But we've heard it at least a million times
All things are possible if we believe
Make no mistake about it
To attain greatness takes a fight for sure
But with God and with the faith to believe
We will achieve if we'll only endure
They say when we do great things with our life
It's our gift back to God
So I admonish you to be all you can
For the dreams for greatness, He placed in our hearts

Poetic Inspirations

Remembering Special Times With Our Mothers

*I remember all my firsts
And you always being there
Helping, listening, encouraging
Showing how much you care
As I ponder the beginning
Of this another year
I'm comforted with the peacefulness
Of knowing that you're still near*

---

*I've learned to love
By watching you
The things you did
And didn't do
Though you're not
The Valentine
Most think of
Still you're mine
My sweetheart
My special friend
The love I want
To never end*

---

*Your love sometimes silent
Reassuring nonetheless
Always giving, always there
Reminding me that I'm blessed
Blessed and abundantly blessed
In so many wonderful and sentimental ways
Blessed just knowing you'll comfort me
Through my dark and dreary days*

Babette Bailey

Showers make things fresh
Showers make things grow
Showers make things livelier
Showers make things whole
You've showered me through the years
You've helped me to become
Wholesome, fresh, lively and more
With all that you have done

You're a beautiful mother
Inside and out
You're strong and wise
You make me proud
Your love is special
In so many ways
Your giving
I really appreciate
I want to say
I want you to hear
I want you to know
That I'm sincere
As I extend
My special thanks
And love to you
This Mother's Day

For summer bugs and summer heats
There's swimming pools and ice cream treats
For missing school and missing friends
There's staying up late and sleeping in
For wishing summers would hurry and end
There's picnic lunches and Disneyland
I've enjoyed summers cause moms like you
Made summer fun from summer blues

Poetic Inspirations

I remember summers in July
Fireworks, hot dogs and fish fries
Corn on the cob and baked beans
Get-togethers with our families
Volleyball and softball games
Boating and swimming across the lake
Lots of fun and lots of food
Lots of laughter, lots to do
Thanks for all you did to make
Our summer holiday memories great

We never missed a beat
You always made a way
We never lacked a thing
No price you wouldn't pay
We needed clothes for school
Shoes and school supplies
And every year, no matter what
We knew we could rely
I'm sure that times got tough
So thanks for holding on
Thanks for never giving up
Even when our thanks didn't show

The sacrifices made for love
Can never be repaid
Sacrifices made by moms
Nothing can replace
The greatest love of all is
When one lays down their life
When I think of all you've done for me
I can't help realize
Your love is that kind of great
For still you sacrifice
Your own desires every day
Still giving your life for mine

Babette Bailey

I used to be afraid of the dark
So you left the nightlight on
And sometimes I had bad dreams
So you held me till the fears were gone
I'm not afraid, not anymore
When I have thoughts that bring me fear
It seems as if I still have the peace
You instilled when you were near

What does Thanksgiving have to do with food
Except for this
We're fed, nourished and satisfied
Just to start the list
Being fed helps you see
There's reason to give thanks
Just think of how you feel
Without eating just one day
And Thanksgiving dinner
Isn't just another meal
It's that extra mile that mothers go
To express how much they feel
So thanks for all your giving
Thanks for all the food
For that which was to nourish
And for all the extras too

What can I get you mom
I just don't have enough
I want to buy you everything
And wrap it up with love
I want to buy you happiness
For all your years of tears
I want to buy your worries
And make them disappear
I want to buy your dreams
And make them all come true
For all your blessings through the years
I want to bless you too
Just know that what I can, I'll do
And know how special you are
And please receive my gift of love
A gift straight from my heart

Unique And Special Roses Collection

The Most Beautiful Rose Of All
Well, I'm a little shy
I know I'm not as pretty as the rest
I'm not as full of charm and beauty
They say, I'm not the best
But I know I still have purpose
I know I still can be
Wonderful and loving,
Gentle, kind and sweet
If you're looking for potential
If you can see past all my flaws
Maybe you can see that inside
I'm the most beautiful rose of them all

My Own Special Rose
What a rose, what a rose
What a sweet and precious rose
And you're mine all mine
I want everyone to know
You're not just another rose
You're my special pick
There were many to choose from
But with you I was convinced
You have just the right aroma
You're just the right size
You have the most grace and beauty
At least in my eyes
I looked at a few others
But they didn't stand a chance
I was totally hooked on you
It was love at first glance

Baby Rose

A baby of a rose
Yet to blossom and grow thorns
Still wrapped tightly in your blanket
All snuggled nice and warm
A beauty rare and sweet
Though with time your beauty will change
From the cute and precious little bud
To the beauty that comes with age

Fine Rose

Today I'm going running
Got to get my exercise
Roses aren't just beautiful
Roses are also fine
I'm going to drink lots of water
I know it's good for me
And get me lots of sunshine
I want the world to see
My rare and lovely character
My style and my grace
And know there's so much more to me
Than just my beautiful face

These Roses These Days

Buds today
Tomorrow blooms
And tomorrows seem
To come too soon
I dare not blink
If I do I might miss
The days of all
Your innocence
These days while you're
As cute as can be
These days while you're little
Is all you need
These days when you're growing
So much inside
These days that will determine
Your tomorrows of life
These days that later
You'll look back on and see
Why I tried to hold you
So close to me
For I know these days
Won't last always
So I'll cherish the memories
Of these roses these days

Old, But Wise Rose

This rose is old but I have much to say
About the loves I've seen in my day
I've seen some loves as strong as an ox
And some that were built on the Solid Rock
I've seen some loves as deep as the deepest well
And some so hot, it could make the heart melt
I've seen some loves you could never understand
And some that came with certain circumstance
I've seen some loves so innocent and pure
Where there was no doubt, they were meant to be for sure
I've seen some loves as sweet as honey from a bee
And some that didn't know a flower from a tree
I've seen some loves go through all kinds of tests
Those grown from day one, were some of the best
I've seen some loves so wonderful they'll make you cry
And some that simply ran out of time

The Roses To Say

Roses are given
Like diamonds and gold
Like pearls and chocolate
So we've been told
Roses are given
As those gifts of love
Those romantic gestures
And special occasions of
Anniversaries and birthdays too
Lovers' day and honeymoons
Forget me nots and I love yous
I'm thinking of yous and promises too
Roses are the ones to say
I love you forever and always

Rosie

My name is Rosie
I'm more than just a rose
I'm a representative of love
I will always let you know
I'll tell you if his love for you
Is genuine and true
I'll tell you if he wants to play
Or if he's serious about you
Now listen very carefully
If you see me again and again
You can almost place your bet
That he's the one you're going to win

Unique Rose

Every rose is unique
In its own special way
In colors and in sizes
In aromas and in shapes
Every rose is tender
And full of beauty and charm
Precious and amazing
Soft and full of warmth
Every rose has class
And a style all its own
And every rose is filled
With potential, destiny and hope

I'm The One

I know I'm the one
I can feel it in my soul
You checking me out, wondering
Who's this fox of a rose
Everything's in tact
From my head to my waist
I smell good, I look good
And I know this is my day
When I woke up this morning
The sun was shining bright
And my petals were stretching
Waking from a beautiful night
I knew that there was something
Extra special about this day
Yes, there was something inside telling me
That you were on your way

Imagine This Rose

Imagine me as your rose
I'm as beautiful as you want me to be
I'm given to you for whatever occasion
Let your imagination run free
I can be long and vibrant
Healthy and very, very cute
Or I can be precious and tender
And expensive too, you choose
I can be a long-awaited promise
Or a very special gift
A warm and heartfelt I love you
Or simply because you're missed
Whatever I am make sure it's special
Cause I'm whatever your heart desires
Sent from that very special someone
Whom you really, really admire

A Man, A Rose?

Can a man be a rose
Well, women love men
And women love roses
So I guess a rose could be a him
Attracted to their aroma
Attracted to their form
And they do make women feel
Some kind of special when they get one
Just know they can be thorny
And you should always handle them with care
Yes, just like a man
So women, always beware
Those roses can be very charming
But be careful that they don't hurt you
Be very careful how you care for them
And they'll compliment your virtue

Colored Roses

Yellow roses are for friends
Red roses are for love
White roses are for peace
And pink roses just because
A single rose say's I'm sorry
Two roses say I do
Half a dozen say smile, don't worry
And a dozen, I'm thinking of you

Next Chapter

You grew from just an infant, went from crawling to standing
From mumbling to chanting, from bouncing to standing
You learned to read and write, learned wrong from right
Learned to stand and fight, learned to embrace your plight

You've gone from chapter to chapter, from one situation to the next
From one song to another, you've always given your best
You've served and you've sacrificed, you put in your time and labor
You're about to begin the next chapter, you're about to start your next adventure

I hope your next chapter is just as impacting as the ones that have made you who you are
I hope your next journey continues to amaze you, and continues to impact your heart
I hope you take time to relax, to always laugh and embrace
I hope you take time to see the sights and the journeys you've always wanted to take

I pray that God will continue to lead you as He has since chapter one
I pray that this next chapter will be all you're hoping for and then some
It's time to be served as you have served, your journey has brought you to this place
It's time for you to reminisce and reflect, to exhale and to embrace

It's time to impart and teach from your experiences, to share from all that you've seen
To give your perspective, your interpretation, your opinion, your insight from what you've gleaned
It's time for your journey to take yet another turn, another door has opened to new opportunities
Be ready to receive more of the things God has for you, to partake of more of His wonderful blessings

Lifting Us

The prodigal son found himself so low
He was eating from the same trough with the swine
But God brought him to himself and he went home to his father
And was given a new start on life
Peter denied Jesus and was filled with remorse
He never imagined he could fall so far away
But God lifted him, restored him, gave him a fresh new anointing
And Peter experienced God's amazing grace
It's amazing how low we can utterly fall
How far we can drift in our mess
How we can go from being ready to give our all
To utter selfishness
We can think we're standing in our strength
And fail to see God's love all around
Till the winds start blowing and the waters start rising
And it seems God is nowhere to be found
It's those times when we're desperately searching and in need
That God's anointing power is released
Those times when we're groping around in the darkness, crying
That God opens our eyes, lets us see
It's not by our might nor by our strength
But the anointing power comes from Him
It frees us to worship with all our heart
With passion and gratefulness, humbly bow
So, thank God for the fresh new anointing
That lifts us back up when we fall
That helps and comforts, strengthens and fills
That equips us and is with us through it all
That breaks and destroys every yoke
Makes us free from oppression and pain
Lord let there be fresh new anointing of Your power
Filling and guiding us every day

Babette Bailey

No Matter What

When it's cold or when it's hot
When it's good and when it's not
In the snow, in the rain
Through life's heartaches and pain
God is there, He won't leave us
Yes, we can count on God's great love
When we're hurting or burdened down
When our loved ones aren't around
When our hopes and dreams delay
When we can't even seem to pray
God is still strong and great
Yes, He's still worthy to be praised
In our achievements and success
When we fail though we've tried our best
When we're pressed on every side
When the storms threaten our lives
God still loves us just the same
Yes, He promised His love would never change
There will always be rainy days and Mondays
Times when we press despite the pain
There will always be sad songs and blue songs
Songs from the wounds of our soul
There will be times when the leaves all fall away
When the sky is dreary and gray
When the cold is bitter and the stars don't align
Times when we just can't help but cry
In every season God is still right there; He's still sovereign and He still cares
Though sometimes it's harder to feel His arms; that's when we must be assured in our hearts
That God is faithful and His words are true, and though He allows us to go through
We can count on His strength and grace, to sustain us no matter what storms we face
Our goal is fighting the good fight of faith; holding on when the seasons change
Believing God when we feel alone; ignoring the pain and standing strong
Endeavoring to love, to serve and give, and to glorify Him in how we live

Walter (AKA – June Bug)

Do you remember him laughing at his own jokes
Always the comedian, always cracking on somebody
Every time we had some kind of get-together
If June Bug was there, he would have us all laughing
Do you remember the musician, his love for music
He had a skill and an ear to hear every instrument
He had a way of bringing all those sounds together
He definitely had a gift and a talent
What about the giver; do you remember how he would give
And so freely, a hundred here a hundred there
If you paid him back that was good, but if you didn't
He might bring it up, but he would still give, he really didn't care
He was a painter, a roofer, could fix cars, a jack of all trades
And though sometimes he came when he could
Most of the time he came right away
If you called him to help you, if something needed fixing
He would help you, even if you couldn't pay
Don't get me wrong, it wasn't all good; everybody knows
That Walt wouldn't hesitate to set you straight
If he disagreed with you, he would definitely let you know
Yau'll know with certain things he didn't even play
But we've all been touched one way or another
By this friend, this dad, this son and this brother
We all have our memories of who he was to us
We all have some wonderful moments we can treasure
To all of his friends and all extended family
Let's hold to some of the lessons from my big brother
Let's keep laughing, sharing, loving, and giving
Let's keep helping and caring for one another
There's one more thing still tugging at my heart
That's where he will spend eternity
Some people believe in heaven and hell, eternal life
Unfortunately, we didn't talk enough about these things
But he's gone and it has definitely shaken us all
We didn't expect it, we've all been just doing our own thing
But I'd like to encourage us to take this time and consider
Our own beliefs and where we want to spend eternity

Babette Bailey

Thanks Goes With Giving

*Thanks goes with giving when you're really grateful
and have a tangible need to respond
When what you feel is greater than thanks
and you must do something above and beyond*

*Giving back is the act that supports the words
that really expresses gratitude
Always say thanks, but if you're more than grateful
then giving you should also include*

*Jesus healed 10 lepers, but only one returned
to show Jesus how grateful he really was
Many say thanks and then go on their way
but others give back to express their love*

*This Thanksgiving families will come together
to show love and appreciation
Cooking, sharing, serving, traveling
and giving beyond the thanks*

*May those you really appreciate
feel the thanks you're giving
May the gifts that you receive be received
as a heartfelt offering*

*May God be pleased with our thanks
may He also be pleased with our giving
May our efforts to go that extra mile
be as God's own personal blessing*

Have A Happy Thanksgiving!!

Poetic Inspirations

Check Your Heart

Is there anyone in your life that needs kindness, patience or forgiveness
Anyone that you can connect God's heart to by simply just being unselfish
Is your heart filled with compassion for those who are hurting or going through
And do you even care to reach out to those with those nasty attitudes
Is your heart concerned for others or are you continually thinking of self
Are your prayers all about you or are you praying for someone else
As we sow, so shall we reap
If love we give, love we receive
Love is a gift worth the giving, though it costs, it's worth the price
Love is a gift that will keep on giving, it will flow from life to life
If you're feeling empty or feeling a void
If there's lack in your life and you feel you need more
Check your giving or what consumes you
Check your heart and look for the truth
Then ask God to show you what you can do
To help, to encourage, to serve, and who
Let go of the wrongs and those hurts of the past
Forgive and then don't dare look back
Reach for God, from the depths of your soul
Let Him have complete control
Let Him fill your heart then move
From heart to heart with the love He gives you
The goal is to reach the hurting and the lost
Tell them of Jesus, that He paid the cost
Give them the hope that we received
Tell them of when you first believed
Let God use you to comfort and bless
Share the light of God's love through the darkness
The void you fill you'll see is yours
Those empty feelings will be restored
The lack that you felt you'll see is gone
Your needs will be met and it won't take long

Babette Bailey

Destination Greatness

Eyes have not seen, ears have not heard
What God has in store for those that keep His Word
No good thing will He ever withhold from us
As we walk upright before Him with confidence and trust
His blessings will overtake us, make us rich and add no sorrow
He'll fill us with hope and dreams of greater tomorrows
Goodness and mercy will follow us all of our days
His blessings are coming to us in unexpected ways
Exceeding and abundantly above what we can ask or think
God is working out for our good, every wonderful thing
By faith we can rejoice for the great things on the way
By faith we can believe and keep looking unto Him day by day
Believing for that breakthrough we know it's on the way
Believing God has the answers, He hears us when we pray
God's gonna show up and show out, it's just a matter of time
As we faint not, but hold on, God's glory is magnified
Keep praying and keep believing
Keep striving and pressing in
We're gonna see the greatness of God
For we have the victory – Yes! We win!

Through The Tests And Trials

I believe that we all have faith, but faith in what and faith in who
We all will have our faith put to the test to see when we're tested what we will do
Our faith should be in God and His Word, not in people and not in things
For He is the one who sees all and knows all, and He holds our destinies
Some of our tests are like little quizzes, they're usually easy and don't last long
But some tests are much more intense and complex, they seem to go on and on
Some tests we've taken again and again, some mountains we've been on way too long
Some battles, some valleys, some struggles and some issues have kept us from standing strong
When the trials come to test our faith; when it seems like all hope is lost
Can we face our trials like the Hebrew boys; trusting God no matter the cost
If we're going to see God's promises fulfilled, if we're gonna enter in and overcome
Let's re-group, re-new, re-position and re-do, and get ready for the abundance
Look at the amazing things God's already done and brought us through
He has given us wonderful miracles and blessed us so wondrously too
But we must fight to hold on to our faith, as we're stretched and enduring through our tests
We must fight to keep hope and faith; we must fight with all we have left
We must fight and not quit and give in, and endure as good soldiers do
When we get knocked down, we must get back up and continue to press our way through
It is a fight and our enemies are fierce; we need our sword, our shields, and all our armor
We need faith, if only a mustard seed to be victorious and to overcome
We're at war but not against flesh and blood; there's a battle raging in our minds
We must fight by the Spirit of God, and by faith we will win every time

Your Race

The training is intense, it's crazy, it's hard; but all you can think about is victory
One more rep, one more step, one more push, one more time,
your body is screaming what are you doing to me
Why does it require so much sacrifice to reach your goals of fulfillment and success
Why must you endure so much pain, what's driving you, why do you want to be the best
The fire of desire, we've all felt that heat, and sometimes the flame can feel out of control
The passionate longing, hopeful determination, that nothings gonna keep you from your goal
Do you not know that in a race all run but only one will get the prize
So we're admonished by God to run in such a way that we will not be denied
Our ultimate goal is to receive the heavenly prize; that which God is calling us to
These earthly exercises are tools and practice runs to show us what we must go through
The training, the failure, the hurts, the emotions, the thoughts of throwing up our hands
Those feeling are only common, we've all been there, but be encouraged they will come to an end
Focus on the finish line, I know it's trying, and it seems like you're so far away
But focus on the training, listen to your coach, encourage yourself, but do whatever it takes
Remember the race is not given to the swift, nor the battle given to the strong
The race, the battle is given to the one who endures and never lets go
Run, press one more time in prayer; one more time in praise
Run, press one more sacrifice; one more time in giving thanks
Run till running gets easier; run when you don't think you can
Run when you're hurting and all wore out; run even when you don't understand
Run whatever the race that God is calling you to; you can make it! Don't give up
Run, God has given you everything you need; just keep your focus on His love

Considering Christmas

Christmas is celebrated by some
As the birthday of Jesus Christ
Christmas is celebrated by others
As a time for giving gifts and surprises
Have you ever stopped to consider
What it's really all about
Why some refuse to celebrate
While others go all out
Have you ever searched for yourself
Have you tried to find the truth
Or do you just go along with the crowd
And do whatever they do
Have you wondered where giving began
Why the stars, the wise men and the lights
There are many mixed emotions, based on this and that
All feel that their way is right
Well, whatever your conclusion
I still say Merry Christmas
I hope you are still filled with peace and joy
And that you and yours are blessed

Babette Bailey

Singing Praises To God

Several are chosen each year for the team
Called from all walks of life
Knitted and fitted together for a season
Each strategically positioned for their plight
Praising and worshiping God is the aim
Melodiously lifting every voice
Playing instruments, dancing and clapping
Making a joyful noise
With one sound and one voice
One purpose to touch God's heart
To bless the Lord, to be on one accord
And to exalt the Lord our God
This season as we're especially filled
With love, warmth and cheer
Let us express our love to the world
Let's let our love fill the air
I pray that our praise and love will grow
That we'll fulfill His plan and reach our goals
As we celebrate the King, the Savior born to us
The greatest gift to the world, the Gift of Love
Let's take our praise to another level
Let's enter into an amazing endeavor
He has given us tools, weapons and keys
He has given us hearts and voices to sing
The gifts are within us that He's calling for
So let's lift them up to our Savior and Lord

Longing

I said I would not long still my soul is in anguish
Longing to feel what lovers feel
I've stood for so long that my knees have grown weak
Longing for love to love me
The pain is so real I can't help but fear
That there's more that I still have to bear
I thought God would surely have come by now
But I can't find Him anywhere
My dreams are fading, losing the hope
That was once so alive in me
Fighting to keep the faith in my heart
Fighting to keep it from grief
I know God will come He won't let me fall
I know God cares, and He hears my call
I'm determined to stand and to pass these tests
I'm determined to keep waiting, I'm doing my best
I know that every good and perfect gift
Comes from God so I'm looking to Him
I can't wait to see what God's going to do
I can't wait to share with you

What Does It Look Like?

Being reconciled to God
What does that look like and what does it mean
I believe it's like the prodigal son who strayed away
And ended up losing everything
He took his inheritance, squandered his wealth
He ended up eating food with the pigs
Ashamed, humiliated and hopeless
How could he even think of going home again
Not knowing that his father was longing for him
And praying for him to come home
He didn't have a clue how much his father loved him
But he had nowhere else to go
Battling in his mind, all he could see was the wrong he had done
He knew he didn't have the right to even ask
He had forfeited his rights, so if he could just be a servant
He wasn't looking for or expecting more than that
As he mustered up the courage and gathered his strength
He had no clue that his father would be overjoyed
So much so that he would celebrate him
And do exceeding and abundantly more
Can you imagine that kind of celebration
All your offenses paid in full and forgotten
Can you imagine your returning could be just like this
If you would just come back to your Father
He wants you to come back home
Whatever you may have done, whatever state you're in
Don't worry what others may think or say
His love is greater than we can comprehend

Poetic Inspirations

I've Been There, Done That

I don't want you to go that way
I know that what you're doing is only gonna bring you pain
I wish I could spare you, I'm trying to reach your soul
But I feel like I'm doing more damage by trying to hold on
I don't know how to make you understand I'm not your enemy
But I've been there, done that, and now that I can see
I just wanna help you and lead you if I can
Away from the destructiveness and the deception of man
I want to encourage you to look unto God
Draw close to Him seek Him and give Him all your heart
Let Him be your anchor, your peace, and your help
Let Him carry you and do what you can't do for yourself
I say to you awaken – awaken, rise and shine
Be awakened to the truth, stop believing all the lies
You're beautiful, you're lovely, but I know you can't see
The insecurity, the rejection, the fear and unbelief
The enemy has done his best to keep you held down
But it's time for you to rise up and to put on your crown
You are royalty, you are rich, you are a wonderful masterpiece
Fearfully crafted by the Lord God, the Almighty
The Creator of the universe wants to show you His love
He wants to shower you with wonderful blessings from above
It doesn't matter how tall, how short, or imperfect you may feel
What matters is that you believe God's power is real
If you lay down your burdens and give Him your plans
Let God lead you, put your hands in His hands
If you can believe, God can open any door
He can do exceedingly and abundantly more
He's a miracle worker, a healer, a deliverer
He's a comforter, a counselor, an ever-present help, a way maker
He is love, He is peace, He is truth, He is light
He's whatever you need, He always shows up right on time
We've heard it all I know a thousand times before
Been there, done that, seen it too, I'm sure
But this time hear it with your heart and ears of faith
This time don't rely on your intellect, don't rely on what you think
This time put it all in God's care
This time believe that God is there
Expect a miracle, Expect your breakthrough
Expect to hear the voice of God, Expect Him to help you
Awaken your spirit, as He knocks, let Him in
Rise and Shine in God's purpose and fulfill His plans

Babette Bailey

Awaken, Rise and Shine

Please let me help you
No, you don't understand
You're always judging me, I don't need you to hold my hand
You're a part of me, I'm sorry that I made you feel that way
When you hurt, I hurt – It hurts me when you're in pain
It seems like to me, you don't give me a chance to grow
Like you want to live my life, like everything I do is wrong
I have no choice, I can't control what you do
But what God has given to me, I want to give to you
He has taught me to understand wrong from right
He has shown me He's the way the truth and the life
He has placed before us life and death
And we must choose and I know His way is best
I've got it, you've only told me a thousand times
I know that you love me and want the best for my life
Now please let me go, you are smothering me
Stop tripping, stop treating me like I'm still a baby
Oh Lord, help me, what else can I do
I know I have to entrust these children to you
Lord you delivered me from my evil ways
So I'm asking for them that You'll do the same
Let them awaken, let them rise, let them shine
Let them see how brilliant and amazing is Your light
Thank You Lord for hearing my plea
As You're working it out Lord, please give me peace
Daughter awaken, rise and shine it's time
Let go of all that stuff, come into the light
Be cleansed, be free, be made whole
Be delivered, you're forgiven, you can come home
Mama, it's me
Baby are you ok
No I'm tired
I'm tired of going my way
Come on in, I've prayed that God would bring you home
Can God really forgive me for all that I've done wrong
I'm a witness that God can forgive because one day He brought me out
Mama you ain't never done no wrong
Girl what you talking 'bout
I've messed up, been jacked up, been tore up and had given up
You mean to tell me, you've been down and out
I've been down and out, wrong and loud, and the one they were talking about
Wow, thank God for Jesus, thank God for mamas
Thank God for children, even with all their drama

Awaken

The Lord knocked but I didn't know it was God
I heard the knock but I didn't see anybody
I called out to hear if anyone was there
But I went right back to sleep because I couldn't hear clear
God was calling to me to wake up oh sleeper
He was trying to awaken me, arouse me from my stupor
From the mess I had made and that I had been in so long
From the suffering and the pain that I was causing on my own
Time and time again, I had cried myself to sleep
He was trying to get me to open my eyes, He wanted me to see
To understand that what I was enduring that it didn't have to be
To see that the person really responsible for hurting me, was me
I had the wrong thinking, the wrong heart and motive, the wrong belief
That's why the pain and the suffering was all that I could see
So for years this vicious cycle, I kept on repeating
I didn't realize for years, God had been trying to awaken me
I cried out to God, not knowing He was already there
I continued to struggle, wondering if God really cared
I felt that He was justified to leave me by myself
All the mistakes I made, all the times I rejected His help
But that was the enemy, that wasn't our wonderful God
Always accusing and telling me what I was and was not
Trying to consume me with guilt and shame
Trying to discourage me and defame my name
I admit there were times satan had me on the ground
Times I was ready to just lay it all down
Times that I was too weary to go another round
Times I questioned what I thought I had found
But now that knock that I had been hearing at the door
Has finally awakened me and I can hear His voice
My eyes can see God is real and how much He cares
I look back and I realize He's always been there
I was in a daze, sleep walking, in some kind of a trance
Doing things my own way, not keeping His commands
But God has awakened me, and the curse has been broken
He has shown me that He is the one I should put my hope in
Not mama, not daddy, not hubby, not a friend
Not fame, not fortune, not job and not my strength
It's time to awaken, It's time to arise and shine
It's morning, It's a beautiful day, It's your season and your time
Make the decision today, to believe and receive
Awaken and arise, be all that God has called you to be

Hope Fading

Wow! I was thinking how broken I am
How confused, how weak and how messed up I am
Everybody else is doing selfies and videos unapologetic
Not worrying about flaws and imperfection, or trying to be fixed
Feeling jacked up in my mind, I've reached out a time or two
I was crying out for help, but I had to just keep pressing through
I wonder who may be in the same place
Reaching out and crying out, feeling trapped
People right around you, talking and interacting
But they can't feel you, they don't know where you're at
You know that something has got to change
That you'll die if you remain the same
But hope and help, where do you even begin
You see how people can hold so much in
Running, trying to escape their own hearts
But still the drugs, the drinks, not even the sex can fulfill
But you've gotta be strong, trying to carry the burdens for everyone else
You're out of answers, even out of love and you're trying to survive yourself
Even God don't seem to be with you and that's really a desperate place
You always thought no matter what, God would make a way
Hope fading, strength fading, your trying to figure out what's really real
Faith is low, money is funny, friends are gone, but still
You have to keep doing all you can to keep your head in the game
You know that God is going to show up and things are going to change
God is faithful, so keep standing believing He's not a man that should lie
He will fulfill all His promises, He'll show up right on time

Getting Ready

Who can we look to when it comes to getting ready
For what we imagine to be a glorious forever
How can we prepare for all the things that will follow
The vows and promises we'll make to each other
There are so many examples good and bad to consider
As we're planning our commitment and union
So many questions that need to be asked
So we'll stand together through all kinds of confusion
There's more to getting ready than pretty gowns and diamond rings
More than tuxedos and honeymoons and all the material things
There's a covenant to consider God calls sacred and never wants us to break
There's sacrifice, submission, surrender
And stands we must make
In good times and bad, riches or poor
In sickness and health, until we are no more
It's not just cliche, they're principles, guidelines
Beliefs within our hearts that will last through all times
Our bodies can no longer be our own
We can no longer be as two but as one
We must always consider one another
To stir up good works - our love
As I think about it, it really sounds glorious, though I know there are those who disagree
But I'm not looking at the challenges and issues that we'll encounter, I'm looking at the sweet victory
This is not for the faint of heart, not for the weak and immature
This is for the faithful, the strong, the bold, and those who have learned to endure
Yeah getting ready for the big I do should not be taken lightly
We should do all we can to prepare ourselves physically, spiritually and mentally

Babette Bailey

Royal Robes

In the Bible days robes signified authority
They were sacred garments made of the purest and finest quality
They were given to show love, greatness and majesty
Given as expressions of favor, honor and royalty
The hem was specially made, also the collar and the waist band
The colors significant, the cut to fit each man
Joseph received a robe made of many colors
Representing the significance and favor of his father's love
Jonathan gave his robe to David, they were best of friends
They vowed to care for each other through thick and thin
He gave his tunic, his sword, his bow and his belt
Jonathan loved David more than he loved himself
The kings had their robes, the Levites and the priests
Those who served and those honored by the king
The prodigal son returned home and received his father's robe
Job received new robes, after he endured the most
The ephods, the bells, and the tunics had their place
The colors were also chosen according to the occasion
There were robes stripped in humility, robes torn in agony
The greatest was the robe dipped in the precious Blood of Jesus
His robe had a train that filled the whole temple
The most amazing, the most holy, the most extraordinary example
From the Father to the Son, whose love never fails
Whose display of love is greater than anyone else
In His royal robe, He sits upon the throne
We bow as His awe and His glory is shown
Just one touch of His robe and our lives are changed
One glimpse of the beauty and the awesome array
The Lord is in His holy temple, let all the world keep silent
Let us honor His presence and give Him holy reverence

Rare And Special

There's a rare and special character trait
I admire about you
I've seen it in great leaders
In our heavenly Father too
I think it's worth acknowledging
Because it is so good
We all don't have this wonderful trait
Even though we all should
With you there's a place in your heart
For who-so-ever-will
Welcomed and equality
Is what you make every person feel
Whoever wants to participate
Whoever wants to serve
You don't see flaws or limitations
You always see value and worth
I don't think it's a strain for you
It's just the way you are
Like it's built inside of you
From a sincere and genuine heart
I know that you've been called
God has filled you with His grace
You always shine, you always stand out
I always see His love on your face
I see the display of your good works
I know you give God all the praise
I hope my light shines half as bright
As the light that you display
Thank you for leading in serving
In gladness and all sincerity
You always smile
It's a rare and special trait
I hope to always see

Few Are Chosen

Many are called, but few are chosen
To serve, to lead, to speak
Many desire to be used by God
But all can't feed God's sheep
God knows the heart; He knows what's in a man
And He knows the end from the beginning
He chooses whom He will; gives them His power and might
And the wisdom and depth of understanding
He says whom He calls, He also predestined
He justifies and He glorifies
He'll take us from faith to faith, and from glory to glory
He'll reveal Himself in and through our lives
So be strong and courageous, for if God be for you
You know the rest, just stand and believe it
Remember to always lean and depend on Him
For He who begun the good work will complete it
As you humbly celebrate and respond to God's call
By giving and surrendering your life
Be encouraged that by trusting and following His plan
He'll give you all you need for this plight
Receive the weight of glory, as others honor you
We honor you, salute you, and respect God's choice
As you share His suffering, you'll share His glory too
We will look to you and reverence you, as you follow God's voice

Happy Anniversary

Your hearts were united
A bond stronger than you imagined
You didn't know love could keep you
You underestimated the power of love's passion

I hope you consider and truly celebrate
How unique and rare is your love
Many have never been where you've been in your love
An amazing journey most only dream of

You've danced, you've laughed
You've shed many tears
Watched over each other and longed for each other
When you couldn't be near

Love is of God
Perfect gifts come from God
So, consider what you have in each other
A portion of God's heart

We celebrate this day with you
We celebrate what God has done
He took two hearts, two lives, two dreams
And beautifully molded them into one

The greatest gift is love
All those special attributes
Think of all the times if you didn't have love
You wouldn't have made it through

As you reflect on what brought you together
In holy matrimony
I hope you smile and embrace each other
Just like you did in the beginning

Celebrating 50 Years

When I think about 50 years
It doesn't seem like a really long time
But when I think about a car 50 years old
I imagine the miles and miles
We really are fearfully and wonderfully made
How we grow is truly amazing
From infants to toddlers, teenagers and adults
How our lives are constantly changing
As we age there are certain birthdays
That seem a little more special than others
Turning one, thirteen, twenty-one, even forty
But fifty, that's a whole 'nother chapter
They say our sight begins to fade
But I think our seeing actually gets clearer
It's true the pace starts to change
But we've learned that faster doesn't always mean better
In this chapter we stop to smell the roses
We notice the little things most don't see
Every day is special, every life is precious
We begin to see the value in everything
How we become the bridges that connect us
We're the connection for the young and the old
From this place we can see, touch, hear
And better relate to them both
This is truly a time for celebration
As we reflect on all that God has done
And all He has yet to do, and complete
In this good work He begun
So here's to 50 wonderful years
To all you've seen and every experience
And here's to many more wonderful years
Of wonder, love, and fulfillment

Poetic Inspirations

Yes We Can

I've been standing at the foot of this mountain trying to figure how in the world I'm gonna get to the other side
Can't see around it, can't see through it, and God only knows what it's gonna take to climb
The enemy is talking loud in my left ear, telling me I can't and I'm foolish to even try to make it
But God's in my right ear saying Yes We Can, tell that mountain to move and go get your promises
I've spoke to the mountain, but it's still in my way, so intimidating, my God this thing is huge
But I've been stuck at this place so long and I'm sick and tired, and somehow I've got to make this sucka move
I realize there's no reasoning, this thing ain't got no heart
And I realize in my own strength that I can't get too far
So I'm looking at God and I'm looking at this mountain, wondering did I hear God clearly is this task for me
But I know it is, cause I can't ignore all these feelings, all these dreams, things inside of me just won't leave
So I keep searching for direction, searching for help
Asking this person and that person, but I feel like I'm by myself
I know I have faith, God's done some miraculous things in my life
And I know if God says I can that it's only a matter of time
I've just got to do all I can, I don't want any more time to be wasted
I know that the promises of God are good, for His goodness I've already tasted
I've felt His wind underneath my wings, seen Him part the Red Sea for me
As I look back over my life, I see how He's kept me from things seen and unseen
The fiery darts of doubt, insecurity and fear
Have threatened me, even pierced me, but God's been right here
So mountain, get out of my way! Mountain you've got to move!
God's got a plan destined for my life, and I've got a job to do
And yes I can make it, I'm equipped and well able
Yes, I can make it, because my God is faithful
Our President Barack Obama has told us over and over again Yes We Can
He showed us, God sent him to give us hope and He's speaking to us through this man
Many are against us, but there's more on our side
Many are laughing and taunting us, but God's already decided
God's glory will be revealed, so let's press our way through
Let's continue to fight the good fight of faith, cause this mountain has got to move
So when the naysayers and doubters tell us we can't; we'll tell them, Yes We Can
When the doctors give up on us and tell us we can't; don't fret, just say, Yes We Can
When the enemy comes against us to tell us we can't; declare by the Blood of Jesus, Yes We Can
Even when those closest to us tell us we can't; tell them with all due respect, Yes We Can

Babette Bailey

I Wanna See You Soar

This time I'm not aiming at your heart, I'm aiming at your potential, I wanna see you soar
Cause I believe in you, don't want to see you held back, held down, or held up any more
I'm telling you now there's always a struggle, there's always some kind of obstacle
But don't you settle for that path of least resistance; don't you do it, not if it's worth fighting for
See the battle gets started in your mind, are you gonna ride that bull? Cause that bull says you ain't
You better know it's gonna take some guts cause that bull is fierce, and ain't nothing in him playing
You are gonna have to wipe those tears from your eyes, get back up and get back in that saddle
You gotta see yourself conquering, beating him, cause that's what it's gonna take to sustain you in this battle
No more giving up, no more giving in
No more quitting when it's tough, you gotta press thru till the end
Yes it hurts, but you gotta ignore the pain
Hit them suckers back, that's what my daddy would say
You've heard the sayings if you ain't gonna dance at the party, you might as well stay home
And if you ain't gonna drive then get off the road, cause somebody's gonna run you over
If you ain't gonna tot, then get off the pot, cause somebody else needs to use it
And don't ever aim a weapon at anyone, if you don't intend to shoot it
I said all that to say this, there's no more business as usual
No more of that should I or shouldn't I; no, all that stuff is old school
No more guessing and second guessing; wait till you're ready then there's no turning back
Learn to embrace the highs and the lows; learn from your mistakes and get the facts
One more thing remember the race is not given to the swift, nor the battle to the strong
But to the one that will endure till the end; the one that will keep on keeping on

Poetic Inspirations
Can You Drink That Cup

Holy women of God, washed in His Blood, yes we can do all things by the power of God's love
I know you have hopes and dreams, desires and promises you're holding on to
And yes you can attain them all, but my friends those things are gonna cost you
That husband you desire, the one that you thought should have come by now
Have you counted the cost, considered the price; are you submitted, can you bow
That longing you have for God, you say He's everything to you
But if He allows you to be tried in the fire and life overwhelms you what will you do
And what about those desires you have for wealth and for success
There's a price for everything in this world, so what will you pay to be the best
These words are not to discourage you, just to make you stop and think
To reconsider not what you want, but the cup from which you must drink
You must wait; can you drink that cup? Sometimes I know you wanna give up
You must be pruned; can you drink that cup? When so many parts of you are being cut
You must be humbled; can you drink that cup? Can He take away your pride
You must learn true love; can you drink that cup? True love is to lay down your life
To be like Christ is to die, to deny yourself and all of your ways
To be holy women of God, you must be broken, redesigned and changed
He said with Him all things are possible, yes; and He'd give you the desires of your heart
But you must give Him everything, your life, your body, and your soul, every part
He knows the way to the Promise Land; the shortest route may not be right
You must trust Him when Pharaoh's behind you, and when there seems no hope in sight
The suffering will develop your character, character hope, and hope a future
And after you've suffered a while, they'll be nothing lacking, nothing you can't do
Yes you can do it, but wait on God's strength
Yes you can attain it, but keep your eyes on Him
You can succeed in all things but trust in His ways
He'll fulfill those dreams just continue to pray
Now in closing I'd like you to think on a few things
Some incidents, some principles, and some things that came to be
Delilah wanted Samson's secret; she kept asking and wouldn't give up
Her motives were not pure of course, but the principles she used were enough
With persistence, belief and unfading determination
A soft voice, a gentle touch, and some female persuasion
She broke him with the strength we've been given to win
If only we would apply them again and again
Now Rachel on the other hand longed to have a child
Jacob tried his best, but couldn't fulfill her desires
She poured her heart out to God, He alone could give her the strength
To hold on through it all, her hope was solely in Him
It didn't happen overnight, for years she tried and she cried
She was at the point of giving up, but God showed up right on time
He spoke to her storm, gave her strength to go on
He opened her womb and before too long
She held that dreamchild she had longed and yearned for
Though it seemed impossible God was able of course
Now as women we have to admit our physical strength won't always get it
Not even our beauty for our beauty is fading, and no, not even all our wit
But I think we can all agree, that God has already done some pretty amazing things
So don't stop believing, don't ever stop reaching and don't ever give up on your dreams

Babette Bailey

We Need You

To our brothers, fathers, uncles and friends
To our husbands, sons and all other men
I've come to make a special plea
To tell you you're one of our greatest needs
So first of all please forgive us ladies
For the trouble that started way back with Adam and Eve
Forgive us for the nagging that pushed you away
Forgive us for the things we said and didn't say
I'm sharing on behalf of all women who agree
We take our share of blame for the troubles we've seen
Forgive us where we've failed to appreciate who you are
You are our knights in shining armor, you are our superstars
Forgive us for the demands we've made to always have things our way
The lists we've made of things we decided could and could not stay
The disrespect, the dishonor, and blatant neglect
For misleading you and ignoring you, there's a lot of things we regret
How can we make it up to you, we need you and we realize
We're laying aside our selfish ways and laying aside our pride
We cannot do it all ourselves, we're not better off alone
The children need you, the dog needs you, you make the house a home
No one and no thing can fill the void you fill in our lives
God knew just what He was doing when He took us from your side
We're bone of your bone and flesh of your flesh
When we're with you we're complete, without you we're less
So on behalf of your sisters, mothers and aunties
Your friends, wives and daughters I plead
Please forgive us and come back home men, we need you

Women On The Front Lines

To the women on the front lines, God has called you for such a time as this
So ladies move out with confidence, for whom the Lord calls, He also equips
You've been hit with the enemy's best, been knocked down and almost out
Yet you've refused to throw in your towel, you've determined to stand your ground
Now there's been some distractions, which caused some strain
Which caused some problems, which caused some delays
Which caused some loss, which caused some confusion
Which caused some conflict, but here's the conclusion
The battle isn't over, so dust yourselves off
Rethink your strategies, consider the costs
The costs...
Our children, our men, our jobs, all our stuff
Our souls, our minds, and as if that's not enough
Our homes, our freedom, our health and our peace
Our family, our friends, our promises and our dreams
Ladies we're gonna have to do everything it takes
Cause when we add it all up, there's just way too much at stake
Yes, we may have to pray a little more, but what's that compared to our peace
We may even have to give a little more, but if it means that we succeed
Let's go!
Dancers to the front lines; intercessors take your positions
Singers tune your voices up; musicians get your equipment
Ushers prepare your greetings; preachers and teachers prepare to sow
Evangelists and missionaries get your bags and get ready to go
Everybody's got a job to do, everybody's on the line
The enemy has underestimated us, for God is on our side
And if God be for us, Who! can be against us, Who! can stand in our way
Who! can defeat us, Who! what's that you say
None, that's right, we win for God has called us for such a time as this
So women on the front lines, put your confidence in Him

The Game

Successful people are tough people, they're willing to pay the cost
They've determined in their minds they're gonna win, they know what it's like to have to say, we lost
Up till now, you've been playing those preseason games, those games that really don't count
You've been preparing yourselves for the real thing, what the game is really all about
It's about self-esteem, character, and having faith
Believing in yourselves and what you portray
It's about loving yourselves and loving each other
And learning to have respect for one another
It's about teamwork and learning to be as one
Giving a hundred percent and not quitting till you're done
You've got to listen to those who've been in your shoes
They can tell you from experience what to do and what not to do
It's about standing when everything inside you has given up
Encouraging yourselves when the times get tough
It's about life, love and yes, it's about God
He gave you the game, cause He knows your heart
It's one of His ways of saying He cares for you
And one of His ways of teaching you His ways too
He likes the challenges and showing off His power
He likes those comebacks in the last half hour
So remember what the game is really all about
It is that life may get hard, but don't get beat by doubt
Learn from every challenge, learn from your mistakes
Keep your head up and your eyes fixed on what's at stake
When it's all said and done, the games over and the season ends
Will you hang your head and say we lost, or will you say we win
God wants you to win, and your souls to rest in peace
On earth and in heaven for all eternity
So play to win always, and in all you strive to do
Believe in the Lord our God and believe in yourselves too

Poetic Inspirations

Sister Girl

They say you don't choose the family you're born into
But the family chooses you
They also say you don't choose most of your troubles
But trouble will find you too
I know one thing on the battlefield of life
The one that I want fighting by my side
Is my sister girl, she knows 'bout that armor
She knows that together our forces are much stronger
She's calling on God, that's our first defense
She knows without Him, we don't stand a chance
She knows how to pray, and that prayer is key
She's armed at all times, not just when there's a need
Her faith is her shield and her breastplates in place
Her sword is sharpened, she sharpens it every day
Her belt is not too big and it's not too small
Her feet run to battle whenever there's a call
She already knows that her hard hat is a must
That's the reason she can stand when the times get tough
She loves you like family; she's been tried and proven
I know if I get wounded, sister girl ain't moving
She's not leaving me to die, trying to save her own self
She's doing all she can; however she can help
She's not to be underestimated, she's not afraid of a good fight
She don't go looking for trouble, but she'll stand for what's right
Yeah, I want somebody on my side, I can trust and love like kin
Somebody like my sister girl, she's more than just a friend
And the thing that I like most is that she's led by the Spirit of God
She sincerely loves and gives and cares, because that's what's in her heart

Babette Bailey

The 6th Man

What do I know about that 6th man? What do I know about the game?
I believe I know a little something 'bout waiting and being ready when it's my time to play
I know you've been waiting for your name to be called, waiting for your chance to shine
Working on your game, your skills, your confidence, and you know it's just a matter of time
You've been underestimated, been sized up, but that's ok, it's all good
It's all in your favor, it's just toughened you up, and helped you believe in yourselves like you should
Now you're more eager, more determined, more aggressive, more educated about the game
You're more relaxed, more effective, more of a threat, somebody's gonna know your name
You're definitely an asset to the team, you have the potential to mess up the enemy's plans
You're ready to give 110 percent, whatever the team needs to advance
But you know what they say, all that talk is cheap, you've got to bring it, you know what you've got to do
So when your name is called, be ready to give your all, let your actions speak for you
I know that love and passion you have for the game won't ever let you quit
It's that driving force that pushes you, even when you're down it says, you can make it!
If you're that 6th man and you realize how much you can add to the game
If you don't mind standing in the gap for others cause you understand just what's at stake
If you're willing to deny yourself and serve and willing to be last if need be
If you know you've been called, chosen and equipped, I know God can use you on the team

Poetic Inspirations

Words of Encouragement

Your heart is heavy, you're all uptight
You're praying that God will show up, come tonight
The pain, the struggle, the agony, the fear
If only God's voice was loud and clear
If only the choices you had to make
Didn't seem like somebody's life was at stake
God promised that He'd never leave or forsake you
He said you could cast all your cares on Him too
So why won't the pain in your heart go away
And why won't God lift your heavy burdens, you've prayed
Where is your peace, and where is your rest
And how did things ever become such a mess
But God is speaking in that still small voice
It's just hard to hear Him over all the other noise
He's saying don't weep, and be not dismayed
For I the Lord am with you, and I'll lead the way
He's saying take courage and be of good cheer
He's saying be strong in Him and do not fear
He's asking you to trust Him for He has a plan
To be still and know that He is God, He's not a man
He says don't you remember all the times before
That He showed you His power, showed you that He is Lord
How He parted the Red Sea and was with you in the fire
How He fought against your enemies and kept you from being devoured
He says He understands for He has been tried too
He's been through all the same things that we're going through
Death, rejection, longing, affliction
Darkness, anguish, temptation and conviction
Sacrifice, loss, weariness and pain
He endured the cross and never once complained
I know with all that we still need His touch
We still need to feel the embrace of His love
So receive that today; see His arms open wide
Let Him fill the void in you; let Him hold you tight
Tell Him all your troubles, and it's ok if you cry
He'll wipe every tear and make everything all right
Be encouraged!

Babette Bailey

The Brother Was Right

I was talking to one of my friends at the game the other day; let me tell yau'll 'bout what was said
Cause I was feeling fed up, my friend thought I was crazy, she was like girl you done bumped your head
She started talking 'bout this brother she met the other night, and how he had it going on
I was like whatever child, just give him a little time and he'll be done moved on
She was like dang why you sound so bitter, they done messed up your love for the game
I told her girl I'm just tired of these same old players, they ain't got no new move anyway
She was like hold up you trying to tell me you out the game for good or just the rest of the season
I told her girl I'm done with these losing teams and I began to list all my reasons
No commitment, no teamwork, no communication
No honesty, no loyalty, and ol' tired conversation
No sacrifice, no compromise, and always selfish ambition
No affection, no appreciation, too many doggone conditions
Then this brother sitting behind me said he couldn't help hearing, said he even agreed with me
We looked at each other, then looked back at this brother; I was like whatever you're selling, I'm not buying
He was like hold up on behalf of the brothers hear me out, cause there's two sides you know to every story
So, I didn't say nothing else, just folded my arms and let him speak and what he said really moved me
He said just like you're looking, we're looking too, and there's some things we're looking for
Like a sense of humor, energy and a good vibe, and we don't like being ignored
He said we're sensitive too, we've got feelings just like you and yes we need some attraction
But there's something we need above all those things, when he said that he really got my attention
He said all these things you want from a man, can God get the same from you
Are you loyal to God, submitted, committed, can He trust you and rely on you too
He said the problem is you're not even all those things you're expecting the man to be
That's why I said you giving up those brothers for all those reasons you mentioned, I could agree
He said the winning people are on the Lord's side, He can train you to be an exceptional player
He said you know yau'll be the main ones fouling anyway, then quick to holla foul on a brother
He said you should try committing yourself to God, and try giving God all your heart
And you should try marrying yourself to Him, giving Him your mind, your soul and your body
Let your money be His, your time be His, let Him teach you how to recognize the counterfeit from what's real
He said unfortunately there are some dogs, some snakes or whatever you want to call 'em
But there's also some others, some brothers who are ready, but yau'll not ready for them
He said try giving all that stuff to God, cause we need yau'll to get yourselves together
And don't be moved unless they say I do, then you won't feel like another failure
I was speechless the rest of the night; I know that's hard for yau'll to believe
But the brother was right and I couldn't say nothing else, all I could do was receive

God's Saving Grace

One day I had a vision I was swimming and God opened my eyes to see
The things that He allowed me to see, weren't lovely at all to me
I saw that I was a sinner, and my life was really a mess
When I saw my heart and my mind, I didn't dare look at anyone else
I wondered how I had missed it, how I had been so blind
How I had been so misled, so messed up in my mind
If you can imagine the deepest darkness, the confusion and the deception
Then you can imagine how lost I was, and how badly I needed direction
I thought everything was ok, but I was way away from the shore
I had grown tired, thirsty and weary, till I couldn't swim anymore
I didn't know how to get back, discouragement was setting in
I looked around everywhere trying to see where were all my friends
I just knew I had gone too far and there was no way anyone could hear me
I didn't have any strength left, not even enough to scream
I thought about my mama, and all of her advice
I thought about all the things that I had done in my life
Then I thought about the things I had been told about Jesus Christ
And I wondered for the first time where I would spend eternal life
Though it seemed all hope was lost, I still cried out for help
I said Jesus please forgive me, save me, and don't let me go to hell
The next thing I knew I was waking up, somehow my life had been spared
I knew this Jesus had to be real; He had showed me that He cared
He delivered me and gave me another chance to live eternally
To have happiness on earth as in heaven, for in Christ I now believe

God Gets The Glory

I'm here to tell you God wants to get the glory in all that we say and in all that we do
He created us for the glory of His name, and He will get the glory He's due
Somebody said, praise on the court! that means even on the court God gets the glory
For it is He who has made us, gave us skills and desires, to everyone He's given a story
God is revealing His glory through all of creation, the sun and the stars, you and me
The thing that we have to remember, is not unto us, but to God be the glory
You see God gets the glory in the good and the bad
You might not have thought about it, but check out these facts
Nebuchadnezzar boasted in himself when God exalted him, and God was not pleased
t he changed his way of thinking and humbled himself, when God brought him down to his knees
Pharaoh oppressed God's people, and God allowed it, but God had a plan
He was setting Pharaoh up for destruction, to show His people the power in His hands
Now Jesus was hung on the cross, persecuted, beaten and despised
The Son of God, how could this be? He has all power, but He chose to die
You see God gets the glory no matter how things may seem
We look at things from a human perspective, but God sees everything
He can see beyond our motives, beyond our pride and our masks
Our weaknesses, mistakes and ignorance, God sees past all that
He sees our tomorrows and yesterdays; who will betray Him, and who's going to stand
He'll destroy us or exalt us according to our choices and according to His perfect plan
So I'm encouraging you, give God the glory; if He's blessing you, give Him the praise
If you're going through, check yourself, check your heart, it may be God standing in your way
I'm telling you God wants to get the glory, on our jobs, in our homes and everywhere we go
He'll fight for us, or He'll fight against us, but He'll get His glory that I know

My Cross

Excuse me, can you help me
Can you please carry my load?
Well you don't have to look at me like that
Just a simple yes or no!
Excuse me, what about you
Can you carry my cross for me?
Oh never mind, just give it here
You look like you've got your own needs!
Lord, what do I do?
I need help and I need direction
I need money, everything's so expensive
And Lord I need some affection
I've got these voids I've tried to fill
But nothing seems to fit
I'm afraid that if I don't get some relief
There's no way that I'm gonna make it
I've heard that those who are weary and heavy burdened
Can come unto You and find rest
So, here I am, just as I am
Can You do something with this mess?
I acknowledge I'm a sinner to say the least
I admit I've failed to believe
But I'm ready now if You'll reconsider
Will You help me and save me please?
Can You wash me, I've been in the pit so long?
Can You rescue me from myself?
I take all the blame for where I am
I'm not blaming anyone else
If there's really some hope, if I really stand a chance
I'm surrendering all, Lord here I am
I humbly bow and make my plea
I'm sorry Lord, please forgive me

Babette Bailey

Take That Bully Out

I got this revelation about fear, I started to recognize it for what it really is
I started to see how it had kept me from reaching my dreams, and how intimidated it made me feel
I could see that fear was the real culprit, it wasn't people standing in my way
It wasn't that I didn't have the hope to believe, it wasn't that I didn't have what it takes
I found out that fear is a big bully, and I determined one day I wasn't giving in
I had about all I was going to take from that bully, and I determined this time I was gonna win
I planted my feet, got me a few stones, I believed that God was on my side and that this battle was on
And sure enough he came at me, with his insults, threats and schemes
I didn't run, didn't back down, wasn't intimated, I just lifted up that name
said in the name and by the authority of Jesus Christ, no weapon formed against me shall prosper in my life
I said I'm an over-comer by the Blood of the Lamb, I said I'm more than a conqueror in God, the I AM
I kept moving forward, kept pressing in, hit fear right in his head, but that wasn't the end
I made sure he wasn't getting up, I took his head in my hand
I let everyone see the evidence that God is greater than any man
And I've come to encourage you, get those dreams off the shelf
Get your stones and go face that bully, tell him God is your help
Be strong and be courageous, aren't you tired of fear and doubt
I come to tell you, you can make it, take that bully out
God is no respecter of persons, He loves us all and wants us all to prosper
But the thief has come to kill, steal, and destroy; your dreams is what he's after
But if you can believe, you shall see, the glory, the glory of God - just believe

Don't You Wanna Go

Don't you wanna go into the presence of the Lord
Sit at His feet, hear Him speak, hear His amazing voice
Feel the love of His arms, protecting you and comforting you
Holding you, carrying you, guiding you and lifting you
Don't you wanna go, into that place called peace
And just rest for a while, let your mind be at ease
Cast all your cares on Him, lay down those heavy burdens
Be free from all anxiety, free from all your worrying
Don't you wanna go where your strength is renewed
Your soul is revived; you're set free from all confusion
Don't you wanna go, don't you wanna hope and dream and rise with inspiration
Run with excitement, with purpose and determination
Don't you wanna live and have life more abundantly
Don't you wanna have good success, be all that you can be
Oh so many are searching for all of these - God's blessings
So many are deceived putting their hope in people and things
Stop looking at the counterfeit, stop believing the lies
There's only one true way; that way is Jesus Christ
Don't you wanna go, don't you wanna see how beautiful life can really be
Look at things from God's perspective, know what He feels and thinks
Let's get into His presence; let's press our way through the crowd
Let's call on His wonderful name; let's lift our voices loud
If you wanna go, He's always waiting; you can enter His presence any time
Just make sure your heart is sincere, and that you have an open mind

Babette Bailey

The Way

It's 3 o'clock in the morning, and you're thinking about that next fix
That bone, that pipe, that sweet thing, that drink, that pornography, that affair or that trick
Fighting in your mind how good it feels, but how bad the after affects can be
And because you've already been at this place so many times before, the decision by now should be easy
But it's still tempting, there's still a war, a battle raging, pulling on your mind
They say call on Jesus, He's a very present help, and that's true but you're weak and so tired
Can't He just take away the desire, the longing, set you free once and for all
You've heard the testimonies how God saved others, but you're wondering can He even hear your call
Take this thorn from my flesh you plead and you cry, Lord help me I don't want to give in
How long Oh Lord, will You be silent you ask; and what have they done that I haven't
Thinking of the struggle and how long you've been in it is discouraging but you know God can bring you out
You've been on this mountain, in this valley, in this desert too long; no more Lord, you just want to shout
Who knows how long the war will be, and who knows when God will step in and save you
And who knows His plans, His purposes, His wisdom for all the things we're going through
The truth is we're all in this battle, and we must all fight the good fight of faith
We all have some things we must overcome, we all have to call on His name
Even Jesus Himself cried out from the torment and pain, as He was going through
He knew in His heart what was the right way, He knew what He had to do
He knew that His flesh had to die, and that it had to be crucified
But He also knew when it was all said and done, He would sit by His Father's side
So go through, endure, and cry it's okay
Call on Jesus; The Truth, The Life, and The Way

Laughter

I remember when we used to laugh
Our hearts were filled with joy
We laughed at everything
But we don't laugh like that anymore
I wanna laugh again; I'm tired of all the tears
I wanna laugh out loud; laugh in the face of fear
I wanna laugh till it hurts; laugh till I cry
I want others to laugh with me; we'll laugh side by side
We've been so serious, so uptight
So worried and so depressed
So bound up, so discouraged
So caught up and oppressed
But I heard a word from God
That's been resounding in my mind
Saying laughter does the heart good
And I think it's 'bout that time
Ecclesiastes says, there's a time for everything
We've had our time to cry, but now it's time for change
So don't worry 'bout the kids, God's babysitting them tonight
Don't worry 'bout the spouse, God's also got them in His sight
Don't worry about the bills, you know they ain't going nowhere
And don't worry 'bout the job; tonight cast all your cares
Remember what used to make you laugh; remember the good times
Remember how good you felt, when those thoughts came to your mind
Just close your eyes for a moment; go ahead and reminisce
Remember the things that brought you joy; the things that you miss
Now determine from this day forth that you're gonna laugh everyday
Determine to think on the good things, and ask for laughter when you pray

Babette Bailey

Men That Matter

It's God's will that none would be lost
So for these men that matter, God paid a cost
They were born in sin, shaped in iniquity
But God said still they matter to me
Teach them My Word and teach them My Way
Invest in their lives that I might be praised
Let the world see just what I can do
By making these men that matter anew

When you don't feel you matter; can't see why you should
When the world has forsaken you; says you're no good
Get it in your spirit men; you matter to God
And He wants to show you how big is His heart
He wants to make you great husbands and dads
Give you opportunities you've never had

Why do you matter? Why does God care?
He hears your cries, He hears your prayers
He wants to use you, your imperfect lives
The foolish things, to shame the wise
So let God reshape you, go with His plan
When you're ready then go and tell all that you can
Your testimonies, your trials and your successes
And let the world see the men that matter at their best

Good News

Just wanted to share with you for I heard the good news
That Jesus not only saves, He gives good gifts too
Our hearts' desires, our dreams come true
There's no limit to what He can and will do
You've waited, you've prayed and now as we see
God has answered you, He has heard your plea
He has smiled on you and in your life
You've seen others receive and now it's your time
It's your time to shout, your time to rejoice
Your time to dance and lift up your voice
It's your time to laugh, your time to sing
It's your name that now has come before the King
For we've come to know every good and perfect gift
Comes from the Lord our God, from Him and only Him
He'll use whom He will to fulfill His plan
But we know that the blessings are coming straight from His hand
So we celebrate with you what God has done
And we pray that the blessings of God have only just begun
And in all that you trust and believe Him for
He'll give you exceedingly and abundantly more

Babette Bailey

Tied Up
Tangled Up
And Wrapped Up

If the roots of your soul are tied up, tangled up and wrapped up in Jesus
You're gonna blossom one day into that magnificent tree
Whatever God has destined you to be
Right now your roots are deep beneath the soil
And no one knows how God is forming you
All you can see is the darkness around you
But one day those roots will produce
You've got to look at the end result
I know you wanted it yesterday, but just wait
No instant gratification, you must go through the process
And the process takes faith
God knows the seasons, He created them
And He knows when it's time for each of you to blossom
But you must be tied up, tangled up and wrapped up in Jesus
For all these things to happen
Now everyone says God has a plan for your life
A good and perfect plan that He Himself has designed
Can you see it? Can you believe it? Are you looking forward to it?
Will you fulfill it? Only you can decide
They say everything worth having is worth fighting for
So get it in your mind now, that you must endure
Equip yourself for the journey, there will be struggles along the way
But thank God that He's always with you, and don't murmur, don't complain
If you really stop and think, there are some reasons for the roots
There are some reasons they're deep beneath the soil
And that they grow the way they do
They're searching for water, they're keeping you grounded
They're feeding on the nutrients; adapting to their surroundings
They're doing all they can to make sure you stay alive
Their sole purpose is to bring you everything you need to thrive
So if you're tied up, tangled up and wrapped up in Jesus
You need to meditate on Him day and night
You need to know His voice, seek Him, trust Him
And walk by faith, not by sight
Get to know your Maker, seek first His Kingdom
And set your affections on things above
Get tied up, tangled up and wrapped up in Jesus
And you'll become the essence of His love

Get Ready

So this is how the virtuous women do it
This is how they spend their time
All dressed up, breakfast and brunch; talking about the love of their lives
Some may see this as just another women's conference
But I see this as another opportunity for every woman to advance
I see this as another investment; the time and the cost
I've made quite a few investments and I can say I've never lost
Every time God's women come together, lives are touched and changed
God always shows up and moves in extraordinary ways
The testimonies shared, give hope and inspiration
It's guaranteed that those of you who have come with an expectation
You won't be disappointed, so open your hearts and your minds
Let's see what's on the heart of God; let's see where He takes us this time
Let's set our expectations high; take the limits off what God can do
Let's receive this Holy impartation, this transformation, this move
We understand there's some shifting going on; there are some ladies ready to deliver
Whatever stage you're in just know, you can't stay there forever
So get ready to move, get ready to advance
Get ready for the next stage, to celebrate and to dance
Get in position for what God has planned
Get ready for manifestation in the land
Get ready for the harvest and for the overflow
WOW women, on your mark, get ready, get set, go!

Babette Bailey

An Even Greater Call

Three times Peter denied Jesus, afraid for his life, afraid to die
When the rooster crowed, Peter's heart broke as Jesus' words came back to his mind
Afterward Jesus asked Peter, do you love Me; of course Peter's answer was yes
He acknowledged his wrong, repented, and now was ready to give Jesus his best
Following Christ isn't always easy, sometimes we know there is fear
Could it make you turn away, deny Him or even risk not having Him near
As disciples, an even greater call, to feed His lambs and to feed His sheep
Especially chosen, justified and equipped to set souls free
On one hand it's an honor, on the other a sacrifice
For though the rewards are glorious, still the prices are high
Seeing addictions and strongholds broken, hearts and lives healed and restored
A child trained in the ways of the Lord, giving hope to the hopeless and more
Seeing miracles, signs and wonders, even hearing the voice of the Lord
Curses, shackles and chains broken, minds renewed and transformed
But also laboring before the Lord, standing sometimes all alone
Crying out and going through your own trials, while still having to be strong
Then after you've encouraged others, you still have to beat your own flesh
So you won't be disqualified for the prize, you strive like everyone else
People looking to you like you're God, how do you handle the praise
You know the glory belongs to God, so you struggle to keep things straight
Do you ever wonder why you, do you ever feel overwhelmed
Are you ever tempted to not depend on God but on yourself
Some think they understand, and others that they can do better
But you've learned that without the anointing of God, they'll be like those sons of Sceva
The main thing is God has called you, and you know His Word cannot fail
He's given you everything and everyone needed for you to prevail
Some to hold up your arms in the battle, some to tell you when you're wrong
Some to care for you when you're wounded, some to help you be strong
Some to stand beside you in the fight and some that will minister to you
He's given you the money, the strength, the faith, the resources and the wisdom too
So continue to run with diligence, the race that's been placed before you
Be assured that He who begun that good work, won't stop till His work is through

Poetic Inspirations

Love, Tell Me Where You Are

Love! Love! Love!
I've been sitting here thinking about love
Trying to find the meaning in my heart
I've been waiting for love, and hoping for love
Love tell me where you are?
Here I am
Where I can't see?
That's because you're thinking about you, not me
What, love, why can't you just make things plain?
OK, first stop searching for me with your brain
Search with your heart, now, what are you looking for?
For some romance, some flowers, and some gifts galore
See, your selfish, always thinking about yourself
Love is being considerate of someone else
Well, how can I love them, if I don't love me?
Of course love yourself, but your priorities
What you give, is what you receive
The seeds you sow, determine what you reap
So giving is receiving is what you're trying to say?
And love is first giving my own heart away?
That's right, just Jesus He gave His life
He loved us so, He was willing to die
Wow, that's deep; but that was Jesus Christ
That's right and He's The Way, The Truth and The Life
He set the example, He paved the way
He is True Love, He is the Agape
So seek His Way, His Truth and His Life
No matter what you're trying to find
And remember your seeds, giving is the key
Thanks love, I've got it now, sow love and love I'll reap
Then when love comes, it won't go
Simply because I don't know how to sow
I can see it now, love overflowing
I won't know whether love is coming or going
Love! Love! Love!

Babette Bailey

Cover Us

Since I'm sharing there's one more thing I'd like to ask before I go
This is for those who are looking at the ladies and considering taking one home
Would you cover us instead of preying on our weaknesses, please don't treat us like whores
Yes we long for your touch and embrace, but to be covered is what we need more
Would you cover us with your gentleness, we've got so many wounds still tender
Would you cover us; our minds hold so many hurtful things we really don't want to remember
Would you consider covering us with real love, not just another rendezvous
Would you consider putting our needs before yours, and dealing with us in Truth
Remember Ruth; she gleaned in Boaz's field, unashamed, she humbly submitted
He protected her and provided for her then made sure that she was well respected
In the evening she went in and laid at his feet, she was vulnerable and in a way she proposed
He covered her, intending her good, and though she could have been, she was not exposed
Instead he set things in order; it spoke volumes to the man that he was
His plans were to cover her and be fully committed; he determined to give her true love
She took a chance on him and was rewarded; what if we take a chance on you
How will you treat us and how will you leave us; feeling cherished or feeling misused
Will you cover us in good times and bad; or for you is it just a game
Will you cover us in sickness and health; or will you only add more to our pain
Will you cover us for richer or poorer; or just look out for your own self
Will you cover us for better or worse; or leave us for somebody else
Yes, to cover us is a great price to pay; I'd like to think of it as a good investment
What you sow in our lives, you'll reap; if your seed is good, then a good inheritance
And yes we've heard a million times, how much men love sex, so let me give you this tip
We love it just as much as you; stroke us right and you'll be surprised what we'll give
We really do want to please you; we really want to be on your team
We want to be your partners, lovers and friends; all we need is for you to agree
We're vulnerable just like a flower; easily bruised if you're not gentle
We'll give you beauty and a sweet aroma if you take care of us; it's just that simple
So one more time, I'm asking you please, to think on what I'm sharing today
We need love, protection, leadership and guidance and we need to be covered God's way
What you plant in us will grow, and we're eager to produce; we're not stupid, worthless or fools
We're a product of the things sown in our hearts, so give us what you want us to produce

We need security - cover us; and to be desired - cover us
We need love - cover us; and respect - cover us
We need affection - cover us; and honesty - cover us
We need patience - cover us; and fulfillment - cover us
If you can hear me - cover us; if you care - cover us
God's Word can't lie; you reap what you sow

Additional Works
by Babette Bailey
* Books of Poetry * Poetic Calendars * Greeting Cards *
* Home Décor / Canvas Prints * Other Writings & Songs of Inspiration *

Please like and follow **Babette's Creative Writing** Facebook page or contact me by email at writeforyourevent@gmail.com. Let's partner for the Gospel's sake: conferences, special events, poetry readings, or study groups.

Discounted bulk book orders are also available. Please email me for more details.

If you would like a specific poem personalized for yourself or a gift, please contact me directly. Various sized prints are available for framing to enhance your home décor.

A Glimpse Into My Heart is a collection of poems sparked by many different people, events, hopes, dreams, issues, and a lot of other things that have touched & impacted Babette's heart in different ways.

Just like our lives, like a good song, or like a fresh new idea that could go on and on in our minds, these glimpses are meant to open the heart, gently lift the heart, and bring a spark to the heart that will go on and on.

Babette is glad to have this opportunity to touch your heart by sharing her heart with you. You will not only be able to relate to many of the poems in *A Glimpse Into My Heart*, but you will be inspired, encouraged, lifted up, smile, and even laugh.

So many times, we feel like we've heard it all before; we've got it all together; we know what we're doing; we're equipped and ready; or like everybody is wrong, except us. We have even experienced times when we didn't want to hear another teaching, another preaching, another prophesy, or another video. We didn't want to read another book, another article, or another story. And we surely didn't want to talk about it anymore!

I want to encourage you to give it another try! Gather the women in your life, and let's embark on a continuous journey together to develop the Ladies First approach to life. This book is a compilation of life experiences, scriptural truths, and authentic thoughts on matters of the heart.

Original Poetic Calendars
by Babette Bailey

*Shipping Available in the U.S.A.
*Please place your order via email: writeforyourevent@gmail.com

$15 Each or 2 for $25
plus shipping

Option 1: 11 x 8.5 inches Saddle Stitch High-Quality Gloss
Option 2: 11 x 8.5 Heavy Weight Matte w/ Comb Binding
(Add $1.00 for Option 2)

Poetic Calendar by Babette Bailey

$10
8.5 x 5.5

www.ingramcontent.com/pod-product-compliance
Lightning Source LLC
Chambersburg PA
CBHW071504070526
44578CB00001B/438